Christmas Tree Pins
O Christmas Tree

Nancy Yunker Trowbridge

4880 Lower Valley Road, Atglen, PA 19310 USA

Notice: All the information in this book, including values, has been compiled from the most reliable resources available. Great care has been taken to eliminate errors and questionable data. However, the possibility of error is always present. The suggested values result from the author's purchases, current dealer prices at antiques shows, books on antiques, and current articles in antiques magazines. The value of jewelry is affected by: the condition, its mark, its desirability, location of sale, clientele, and demand. Neither the author nor the publisher is responsible for losses or gains which might be incurred from consulting this book.

Cover design by Jerry Trowbridge
Photography by Jerry Trowbridge and Bruce Waters
Front cover: The 12 pins are as follows: Brooks, Bauer, Cini, Carnegie, Mylu, Ballou, Hollycraft, Beatrix, Kirk's Folly, Donna Susanne, Bijoux-Stearn, and B.W.

Copyright © 2002 by Nancy Yunker Trowbridge
Library of Congress Control Number: 2002107093

Designed by John P. Cheek
Type set in Florens LP/Humanist 521 BT
ISBN: 0-7643-1656-7
Printed in China
1 2 3 4

Published by Schiffer Publishing Ltd.
4880 Lower Valley Road
Atglen, PA 19310
Phone: (610) 593-1777; Fax: (610) 593-2002
E-mail: Schifferbk@aol.com
Please visit our web site catalog at **www.schifferbooks.com**
We are always looking for people to write books on new and related subjects. If you have an idea for a book please contact us at the above address.

This book may be purchased from the publisher.
Include $3.95 for shipping.
Please try your bookstore first.
You may write for a free catalog.

In Europe, Schiffer books are distributed by
Bushwood Books
6 Marksbury Ave.
Kew Gardens
Surrey TW9 4JF England
Phone: 44 (0) 20 8392-8585; Fax: 44 (0) 20 8392-9876
E-mail: Bushwd@aol.com
Free postage in the U.K., Europe; air mail at cost.

Contents

Acknowledgments

Thanks to the following people who graciously gave of their time to help me with my book: Donna Anderson of "Donna Suzanne," Dorothy Bauer, John L. Catalano, Jeanne Cavadini for Mel Lyons, Shirley Garness of "Lysa," Wendi Gell, Esme Hecht, Alexis Watts, and Miriam Gibbons of "Lunch at the Ritz," Fran B. Hurst, Ivy Doe Doe for "Anka," Judith Jurgensen, Jenniefer Kirk of "Kirk's Folly," Ray LeVin and Herb Bushati of "Park Lane," Karen in Guest Relations at "Longaberger," David Mandell of "The Show Must Go On," Bobbi Mathis, BeeGee McBride of the "Southwest Texas Trading Company," Steven Miner and Yai of "Cristobal-London," Barb Newman, Sarah Zapf of "Roman," Lou Slovek, Bettina von Walhof, Larry Vrba, Gina Wheeler, Joyce Yost of "JD/DJ," and the "Zarah" Company.

A very special thanks to Rita Eldridge of "Treasures in the Attic" who I met in my early collecting days. Over time, she has become one of my best friends. She has been actively involved in my collection and this book. Her enthusiasm and belief in this project has never waned. I would like to mention the following people who have made it possible for me to find the missing pieces I needed for my collection, as well as answered many of my questions: Laurel Bailey, Ann and Mark Bernard of "The Jewelry Lady & Co.," Kathy Flood of "The Jeweled Forest," Marcia and Mark Lloyd of "M&M Collectibles," Marilyn Jackson of "Uncle Sam's Country Store," Gerry Kempe of "Carrie Richmond Antiques, Inc.," Ann Mills of "Collections by Ann," Steve Peterson of the "Jay Garment Antique Mall," and Jeannie Richardson of "The Betty Boop Gal." Thanks to John Godfrey and Doug Sophia of Godfrey Jewelers for all their help. Many thanks to my friend and associate Bobbi Mathis who loves the computer. Before I bought my computer, she searched endlessly for pins on the internet for me. Also, thanks to our son Ryan who bought all of our equipment for us for this project. He has spent many long hours on the phone with us (between California and Michigan) to help solve our computer problems and questions. And to my editor, Nancy Schiffer, the word "thanks" is not enough! I have truly appreciated the confidence and support she has shown me, and belief that this could be something "special." To the "Schiffer Family" at Atglen, thanks for all the kindnesses you showed Jerry and me while we were there. You made us feel very special! Last, but certainly not least, to my husband, Jerry, who has given endless hours to this book. He has helped search, find, buy, design, and manage this project. Thanks to his love for me and his many talents, this dream of mine has come true!

Introduction

As a child, one of the happiest days of the year was Christmas. It was so exciting: the waiting and wondering, plus the colors and the smells. One knew the season was on its way when we put up our Christmas tree. It was so beautiful with its colored lights, shiny balls, and the pungent smell of the pine tree itself. Of course, there were all the gifts under the tree, too. What wonderful memories!

These memories are still vivid today. As a jewelry buff, I became aware of the beautiful Christmas tree pins I saw ladies wearing on their coats. With memories of our Christmas trees, along with my love of jewelry, I was drawn to the idea of searching for a tree or two to wear myself. Besides, I needed something new to collect, and Christmas tree pins were small, beautiful, and fun to wear. That was the start of something that became an obsession which has turned into a collection of over 1700 pins.

Since I am an elementary school music teacher, I start wearing my treasures the day after Thanksgiving. Every day I cover my blazer with as many trees as possible. One pin is never enough when there are so many to share. My students, as well as my colleagues, have fun seeing the different trees and trying to decide which one is their favorite. I'm sure it is different for each collector.

O Christmas tree, thank you for all the wonderful memories you bring to each of us.

Fall, 2002

O Christmas Tree

1

O Christmas tree, O Christmas tree,
With lush green boughs unchanging-
Green when the summer sun is bright,
And when the forest's cold and white.
O Christmas tree, O Christmas tree,
With lush green boughs unchanging!

2

O Christmas tree, O Christmas tree,
Here once again to awe us,
You bear round fruit of Christmas past,
Spun out of silver, gold and glass.
O Christmas tree, O Christmas tree,
Here once again to awe us.

3

O Christmas tree, O Christmas tree,
We gladly bid you welcome.
A pyramid of light you seem,
a galaxy of stars that gleam.
O Christmas tree, O Christmas tree,
We gladly bid you welcome.

4

O Christmas tree, O Christmas tree,
You fill the air with fragarance.
You shrink to very tiny size,
Reflected in the children's eyes.
O Christmas tree, O Christmas tree,
You fill the air with fragarance.

5

O Christmas tree, O Christmas tree,
What presents do you shelter?
Rich wrappings hide the gifts from sight,
Done up in bows and tight.
O Christmas tree, O Christmas tree,
What presents do you shelter?

6

O Christmas tree, O Christmas tree,
Your green limbs teach a lesson:
That constancy and faithful cheer
Are gifts to cherish all the year.
O Christmas tree, O Christmas tree,
Your green limbs teach a lesson.

Old German Carol

Part 1

Signed Christmas Tree Pins

AAI
1930 ~ 1999

AAI and Accessocraft have the same mailing address. Accessocraft makes the beautiful high quality tree pins while AAI makes unique inexpense trees.

A simple tree whose outline is in green enamel with a little red star on top. 2-3/8" x 2". $15-25.

A small tree using red and green enamel in a zig zag design. 1999. 1-3/4" x 1". $5-10.
A green enamel tree with red stars and chili peppers. Same design, in gold, sold at Target in 1998. 1-3/4" x 1-1/2". $10-15.

Accessocraft
1930 ~ 1998

Accessocraft was founded by Edgar Rodeheimer and Theodore Steinman around 1930.

Two little projectile branch trees by Accessocraft. Each is decorated with glass beads (red and green glass balls, or white glass barrels) that dangle off the branches. Red and green stones are set down the spine of the trees. 1-1/2" x 1". $45-75 each.

This tree has six tiers of red enamel circles alternating in size. 2" x 3/4". $10-15.

A.G.C.

© AGC INC
MADE IN CHINA
Fabrique en Chine

The American Greeting Card Co. tree was made in China. The green tree is made of molded plastic and decorated with multi-colored stars and balls. It has a large red and gold bow across the bottom. 2-3/8" x 1-3/4". $3-5.

This is a musical tree in sparkling green enamel. Reminds one of a pine cone. 2-5/8" x 2-1/16". $45-60.

A tree which is textured and uses green enamel.. It has red enamel bows and a gold garland. Note its star. 2-1/2" x 1-3/8". $30-45.

A.J.C.
1990s ~ 2002

A simple green enameled tree with red enameled balls on each tier. 2-3/8" x 1-1/2". $25-40.

The A.J.C. green enamel tree has red balls with Santa leaning on it. Santa is in red and white enamel. 1998 issue. 2-1/8" x 1-1/2". $10-15.

A ribbon tree with one side in sparkling green enamel and the other in gold tone. 2-3/8" x 1-3/8". $25-40.

These two angel trees are very similar in design. The green tree is not marked. 2-1/4" x 1-3/8". $25-40.
The gold tree is marked "A.J.C." 2-3/8" x 1-3/8". $25-40.

A tree filled with tiny rhinestones decorated with enamel garlands. 1-1/2" x 1-1/4". $60-75.

A jaunty cat holding a tree with red and green stones. 1999. 2-1/8" x 1-1/4". $10-20.

Two cats with tails entwined, sit lovingly in front of the Christmas tree. 3-1/8" x 1-3/4". $15-25.

This tree has four tiers of green crystals that are embellished with a rhinestone garland. 1-5/8" x 1-1/4". $60-75.

This brushed gold sedan has a green enamel tree secured to it's top by a gold textured rope. 1998 issue. 2-7/8" x 1-1/2". $10-15.

Alpha of Britain
1972 - 1998

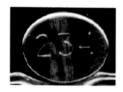

Alpha has been bought out by the Swarovski Company as of the middle of 1998. Alpha trees are beautifully made. They are highly sought after and collectible.

Alpha trees are marked with the register number 234. Each tree comes with a metal tag with the Alpha script "a" on it, plus a paper tag that says "ALPHA". Made in Britain.

A rhinestone tree with tiers of cut out, open branches which are set with rhinestones. 1-1/2" x 1-3/8". $60-75.

Anka
1980 - 2002

Anka is an artist who was born in Novistad on the shores of the Danube River in Eastern Europe near the Hungarian border. She came to America 20 years ago and began designing costume jewelry.

Anka enjoys working with the many possibilities of new materials such as glass, plastic, and bakelite. She uses old and new pieces, mixing them together to create exciting new jewelry which appeals to a wide range of people. Each piece of jewelry is handmade using wire, but no soldering.

Anka's jewelry is sold all over the world including USA, England, France, and Austria. She has now found her place as a valued creator of collectible jewelry. (*Ivy Doe Doe, 1999*)

Anka creates her trees out of pieces of old and new jewelry. This tree pin has an angel with a crown (rhinestones decorate the crown and angel's face), an enameled package, three bells, dimensional glass flowers, and glass beads. 4-1/8" x 2-3/8". $95-135.

Here is an interesting tree with many different circles of colored glass edged in gold. Each piece of glass is a petal of a flower which fills the tree. The top flower has many tiny rhinestones shooting out from the center like fireworks. The tree's trunk is wrapped in tiny glass beads. Hanging off the trunk are five bells and an angel. 1999. 5" x 2-1/4". $100-135.

Art
1950 - 1980

Information on Art is very limited. The Art trademark was used by a number of companies. However, Art Mode Jewelry Creations Inc. was founded in the 1940's. Some researchers feel that Art might have been a separate division of Capri.

This tree is a dark brass color with a slight sprinkle of snow on its swooping branches. White enamel candles (12) decorate the tree with tiny rhinestone flames. This pot design is one used frequently by Art. 2-1/4" x 1-3/8". $50-65.

This tree is created from silver metal with two different pot designs and different colored baguette candles with matching flames. Unmarked. 2-1/4" x 1-3/8". $35-50.

This tree has colored baguette candles with matching flames. 2-1/4" x 1-3/8". $35-50.

A silver tree with branches hanging downward using orange (7), and blue (7) stones. 2-1/2" x 1-3/8". $50-65.

A style often used by Art with layered branches decorated with multi-colored stones (15). 2-1/4" x 1-1/2". $50-65.

A red enamel cone set with multi-colored stones (7). Marked. 2-1/4" x 1-1/16". $55-75.

Another red enamel cone design which is decorated with gold braid and light green stones (4). Unmarked. 2-1/4" x 1-1/6". $55-75.

These cone shaped trees are in heavy red or white enamel. Two arms of gold curve downward from the top star and join at the middle with star "hands." This design was also used for a candle and a bell pin. These trees have a flat triangular base. 2-1/4" x 1". $45-60.

A solid outlined tree with two layers of branches with a fine lacy design. It uses small baguette candles (6) with no flames. Two sizes of stones sit "on" the bottom branches and "off" the top layer. 2-1/4" x 1-1/2". $50-65.

Two layers of prickly branches reaching upward. Tiny orange and green sets are sprinkled over the tree with one blue set at the top under the star. 2-1/2" x 1-3/8". $50-65.

These three trees are identical in design, but the left one is antique gold and sprinkled with snow, using red, blue, and green stones set in an open squashed heart shape. The silver tree in the center has dark blue sets except for the star on top which has an orange stone. The tree at right is a gold metal base with yellow enamel using orange, blue, and amber stones. All have silver or gold balls as part of the decoration. 2-1/4" x 2". $45-60 each.

A dark silver tree with two layers of branches which swoop downward and out. A bit of snow dusts the tree's edges. The usual Art stone colors (16) sit on top of the branches. 2 -1/4" x 1-5/8". $50-65.

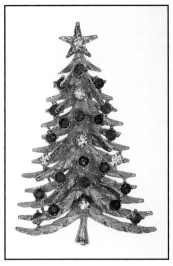

A large tree (Mylu also uses this design) with two layers of projectile branches, using the traditional colors of red, green, and clear stones (22). 2-1/2" x 1-5/8". $75-90.

A small tree with projectile branches holding white enamel candles (10) with tiny colored stones for flames. 2" x 1-3/8". $35-45.

Sometimes known as the "Garland Tree", a garland wraps around this tree set with small Art- colored stones (19). The branches, in a yellow green enamel, swoop down with a sprinkle of snow. 2-1/8" x 1-1/4". $40-55.

Here are four identically styled trees but with different snowy branches. The first has light snow. The second has whiter and heavier snow, while the third and fourth have snow that looks like it is actually on top of the branches. The first tree has a pot which is slightly enameled, while the second tree is darker green enamel with the pot totally colored. The first and second trees use exactly the same color of stones (30). The third and fourth trees have metal showing. The fourth is of brighter metal and looks newer. 2-7/16" x 1-3/8". $40-55.

This yellow green enamel tree has a solid body with the edges of each tier slightly raised and tipped with snow. Orange and blue stones (11) sit on the branches. 2-1/4" x 1-1/4". $40-55.

A double layer of green enameled branches is decorated with red, blue, gold and clear sets (17). An interesting three pronged trunk. 1-1/2" x 2-1/2". $65-75.

Art To Wear
ExClaymations!!
~ 2002

Art To Wear tree pins are made of hand-crafted clay, then glazed and trimmed with 22k gold. 1999. A. 2-1/2" x 2". $30-40. B. 2-5/8" x 2". $30-40.

Attruia
1999 ~ 2002

Attruia's first name is Anthony. He has been with the Swarovski Company for many years. He has also designed and created pieces of his own using Swarovski crystals. This is why it is hard to know if a pin that looks like a Swarovski is the company's without a tag, or, is one of Anthony's. Just now has he started marking his own pieces with a castle logo and his name. I understand that he is always remarking that his home is his castle. Several pieces, in the Swarovski section of the book, are by Anthony, but they are unmarked, so it looks like they might be Swarovski pins without their tags.

Attruia has been designing on his own for many years, but not officially signing them until 1999. His signature is a castle with his name, Attruia, underneath it.

2-5/8" x 1-3/4". $45-55.

2-7/8" x 1-5/8". $35-50.

2 -3/8" x 1-1/4". $45-55.

Cowboy style tree set with rhinestones. It is decorated with a hat and a pair of boots in gold and rhinestones. A garland of red, green, and amber stones are strung across the tree. It has a very fancy tree topper in gold and crystal. 1999. 2-3/4" x 1-7/8". $50-65.

Attruia (Unmarked)

Here are three trees using the same basic design. They are unmarked, but created by Attruia.

A magenta crystal tree with an amber garland. On top is a gold filigree ball. Stunning due to the colors. 2-3/4" x 1-1/2". $40-75.

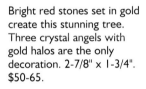

Bright red stones set in gold create this stunning tree. Three crystal angels with gold halos are the only decoration. 2-7/8" x 1-3/4". $50-65.

A basic Swarovski tree design in clear crystals. However, it is unique in that it has a small green tree on it's body which dangles, plus two crystal angels. 3-1/8" x 1-1/2". $40-75.

An emerald green tree pronged in gold. Three gold angels decorate the edges. On the top of the tree is an angel set in front of a tipped square outlined in rhinestones. 3-1/2" x 1-7/8". $50-65.

A most unusual red crystal tree that uses red aurora borealis stones. 2-3/4" x 1-3/4" $70-90.

A big pin whose colors are dynamic. Individual branches are set with emerald green crystals (40). Ruby red stones (6) go down the tree's spine. Small red and clear stones hang between the branches. Amber baguette candles (6) with crystal flames dot the edge of six branches. A large clear pear sits on top. Pronged. 3-1/8" x 2-3/8". $60-75.

Made in Austria

A beautiful old Austrian tree made with seven candles. Each candle is made with yellow and white Austrian crystals. The tree is pot metal with green enamel. Red rhinestones run down the trunk. 2-1/2" x 1-1/2". $150-200.

Another ruby red tree with 57 stones. The branches arch downward. Aurora borealis stones (10) give highlights to this tree. A typical pear stone sits at the top. Pronged. 3-3/4" x 2-1/2". $60-75.

A wonderful old tree whose sweeping branches are set with green and red stones. The candles are clear round crystals with a gold flame which are strung by a pin. 2-1/2" x 2". $120-150.

This Attruia pin has green crystals (68) and ruby crystals (26). Pronged. 1999. 2-3/4" x 1-1/2". $60-75.

A tree created by pearshaped crystals (16) in brown, bluegray, yellow green, pink and clear. A ring of rhinestones encircle the top pearshaped stone. 2-1/4" x 1-5/8". $85-100.

This tree is similar to the classic Weiss five candle tree. 2-1/2" x 1-1/2". $150-200.

Identically styled trees using pearls and colored stones. 1-1/2" x 1-1/8". $35- 45 each.

An interesting candle stacked tree with amber flames. 1-3/4" x 1-1/4". $60-75.

This is the oldest tree of the three shown here. Some have japanned backs. This tree uses small dark green stones with tiny white candles with colored flames. 2-1/4" x 1-7/8". $75-100.

Traditional tree in six tiers using small crystals. 1-1/2" x 1-1/4". $45-55.

A bushy three dimensional tree with red and green dangles (4). 1-5/8" x 1". $60-70.

Avanté

A holly tree with green wash, red stone berries (13), and clear rhinestones (4). Marked on red card only. 2-1/2" x 1-3/4". $30-45.

A slightly concave and cut out tree set with stones (9). 2-1/2" x 1-7/8". $25-35.

Simple molded tree in five layers. Traditional stone colors (11). 2-3/8" x 1-5/8". $25-35.

Avon
1950 ~ 2002

Avon was founded in 1886 as a perfume company. The Avon line was introduced in the 1920s, and then changed the name in 1939 to Avon Products.

This is an open woven design. One tiny rhinestone sits on top. 1-1/4" x 3/4". $20-45.

A molded plastic tree with red roses (13) and pearls (10). It has a mesh white bow on bottom. China: 2001. Unmarked. Marked on box. 3-1/2" x 2". $15-20.

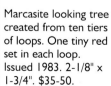

Marcasite looking tree created from ten tiers of loops. One tiny red set in each loop. Issued 1983. 2-1/8" x 1-3/4". $35-50.

Tiers of green enameled branches edged with white snow. Red glass balls (8) dangle off each branch. 2000. 2-3/8" x 1-3/8". $15-25.

Tiny silver lapel pin in a cut out design. 7/8" x 5/8". $10-15.

A bow tree with aurora boreaus sets (6). This is the oldest tree shown here, made before 1978. 2-1/4" x 1-5/8". $30-45.

B.A. Ballou
1876 ~ 2002

The B. A. Ballou & Co. was established in 1876. Currently in Providence, Rhode Island, the company has always been known for quality jewelry.

A beautifully flowing spiral tree. Sold by Ballou, it was also distributed by The Museum Company. 1999. Made of sterling silver or vermeil. Mark: Ballou or Sterling BAB. 1-1/2" x 1-3/8". $30-40.

Dorothy Bauer
1981 ~ 2002

Dorothy Bauer has been involved with some form of art since kindergarten. This interest, and then love, led to an undergraduate degree in ceramics. This was followed by a MFA (Masters of Fine Arts) in glass and sculpture from the California College of Arts in 1981.

Her early plans were to become a sculptor but she needed money to support her studio. Having grown up in retail (her father owned a toy store), she created and sold hand-blown glass jewelry to help pay her bills. It was then she discovered faceted colored crystal. This opened up a whole new world of possibilities for her. She used the crystals to create a line of wearable sculpture.

In 1981, she established her own company called "A Piece of the Rainbow." In January of 1999, the company was dissolved and became known as Dorothy Bauer Designs. Dorothy is the president of the company, her husband Robert is the engineer and business manager, and there are seven craft people who help her.

Unlike many other jewelry companies, each piece is constructed and soldered; each stone is set. Then, each piece is electroplated with fine silver or 24k gold. Only first quality Austrian crystals are used. Her pieces sparkle. Every piece of jewelry can be made in many colors. One year a piece may be made with one color combination and then brought back later in another color combination.

Her designs over the years have become more dimensional. She started designing Christmas trees in 1981. To date she has made 317 different trees using different colors and finishes. She loves designing trees because of their complexity and design. The tree which has been most popular is her XTRD1 tree with the garland. She does this tree in 40 different ways. Inspiration for her designs comes from nature, life, and humor. This is why a Bauer piece of jewelry is always glitzy, fun, and wonderful.

Each Limited Edition piece of Bauer jewelry comes in its own black velvet bag and includes a card of authenticity to record the date purchased.

The color combination in this tree of citrine garlands and purple hearts (11) is truly dynamic. A clear pear sits on top. Limited Edition. 41/50. 2000. 3-3/8" x 2-1/2". $175-225.

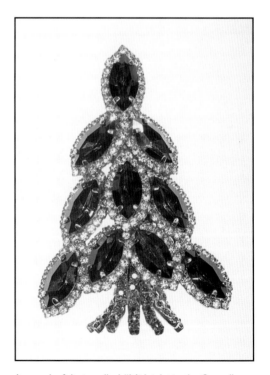

A wonderful pin called "Midnight in the Snow". Midnight blue navettes surrounded by clear rhinestones. Real dazzle and depth of color. Pronged. 2001. Ltd. Ed. 7/25. 3-1/4" x 2-1/4". $350-400.

All trees are very glitzy and have bales so they can be worn on a chain around the neck. This one is sometimes referred to as the "Garland Tree" since each half tier is slightly dipped and underlined with a garland of clear rhinestones. A large chaton sits in a stylized star frame. Pronged. 2-3/4" x 1-7/8". $80 -100.

Two trees which can stand up as an ornament, be strung on a chain, or be worn as a pin. Two layers of branches swooping downward are set with beautiful red and green stones, and, green with pastel stones. A tiny clear rhinestone adorns the tip of each branch. The base is cone shaped and grooved with a ring of stones around it. One is on a silver backing, the other is on gold. Pronged. 1990s. 2-1/2" x 1-3/4". $155-180 each.

What glitter! Each branch is a line of sparkling rhinestones. Here and there are other multi-colored balls (19). Another large chaton sits on top. Pronged. 2-1/8" x 2-1/8". $100 -125.

Lime green stones are set in gold with four clear baguette candles. The flames are red, blue, orange, and green. Pronged. 1990s. 2" x 1-5/8". $125-160.

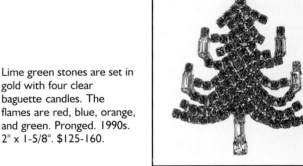

"Rivoli Tree Pin." Here are ten round cut stones which have iridescent colors due to the use of "special effects salt." One clear stone sits at the tree's base. This tree is very convex and is on silver. Pronged. 1999. Limited Edition: 8/11. 3-1/4" x 2". $100-200.

A stand-up tree made of six tiers of green crystal flowers with red centers. Each tier is outlined with a rhinestone garland. A rhine-stone butterfly sits on top. Pronged. 2000. 2-3/4" x 1-1/4". $80-95.

This tree is often referred to as the "Zigzag" tree because of the red "Z" garland across the green body. The top stone is creatively mounted. Pronged. 1-3/4" x 1-1/8". $45-55.

While many current designers are designing large Christmas tree pins, Bauer has designed a Limited Edition line for the 2000 season which is smaller. This tree uses citrine Swaroviski crystals with magenta candles. Pronged. Limited Edition: 20/120. 1-7/8" x 1-7/8". $125-150.

"Be There or Be Square." Here is a dazzling piece. Crystals, squares, and rounds highlighted with vibrant red stones. This tree has a frosted trunk on a rhinestone base. A large ruby star sits on top. Pronged. 1999. Limited Edition: 36/100. 4-3/4" x 3". $125-175.

"Noel Olé." Here is a wonderful tree to be enjoyed all year round as an "object of art"! Emerald navettes create six tiers using different sizes, shapes, and colors of stones for decoration. A rhinestone garland is strung across each tier. At the bottom are four dangling rhinestone balls. The star and the base are filled with rhinestones. Tree was also made with purple navettes. 1999. 24K. Pronged. Limited Edition: 22/250. 3-7/8" x 2 -5/8". $150-225.

"Eiffel Tower Poodle Pin." The Eiffel tower becomes a Christmas tree set with green stones on gold. A light pink and green garland winds from top to bottom. It holds three frosted glass poodle dogs. Three larger pink balls highlight the tree's green stones. A large rhinestone star, in a cut-out design, sits on top. What a sense of humor! Pronged. 1999. 4-1/8" x 1-3/4". $55-100.

2000 MILLENNIUM TREE, 1999. What a wonderful way to celebrate the millennium with this 2000 Christmas tree. Here the number 2000 acts like separate tiers garnished by pastel crystal garlands. A pear drop crystal angel adorns the top holding up 2000 once again. It has its own stand so it can be enjoyed over and over. 24K. 3-1/2" x 1-3/4". $70-150.

Detail of tree bottom.

"Christmas In July." Little glass amethyst flowers with aurora borealis centers create this tree. It has a rhinestone trunk, the flowers rotate, and this flower tree sits on a stand so one can enjoy Christmas in July. 1999. 2-1/8" x 1-1/4". $80-95.

Here is an Art Deco design using ruby rounds outlined in clear crystals. Set in 24K. Pronged. 1-3/4" x 1-1/4". $55-70.

A sparkling little lapel pin with an unusual type of stone. One stone creates the entire body of this tree. A clear rhinestone fits in the trunk and another is used for the star on top. 24K. Pronged. 1999. 1-5/8" x 1". $50-65.

Beatrix
1946 ~1975

Beatrix was founded by Nat Sugarman in 1946. Sugarman named the company after his sister, Beatrice. In 1975, the company changed hands and the name was changed to "B.J." meaning "Beatrix's Jewels."

"Doggone Christmas Tree." Dog bones are all over this tree (even the trunk is the end of a bone). The star is a paw print. It even has its own dog house. Antique gold backing. Pronged. 1999. 3-3/8" x 1-7/8". $45-135.

Identical trees (one in a green wash, the other in gold tone) whose branches spread downward in a flare ending in a jeweled star (8). Note the pronged trunk with a little horizontal band across it. 2-1/4" x 1-3/4". $55-75.

"Large Christmas Tree." Here are 13 tiers of dark green crystals with 26 multi-colored stones. A wire star has a clear crystal stone. The pot has black crystals. Pronged. 1999. 2-3/8" x 1-3/4". $50-65.

Seven leafy branches spread up and out ending in a seven point flower. Each flower has a jeweled center (8). The tree's top uses just three points of a star. 2-1/4" x 1-1/2". $45-65.

"Wagon With Christmas Tree." Here is the little red wagon that some of us grew up with. Even the wheels turn. A smaller version of the "large Christmas tree" is carried in the wagon. Pronged. 1999. 1-5/8" x 2-1/2". $65-105.

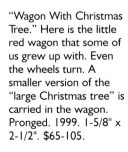

A stylized tree (in a green wash) and deer (in polished metal). The only stones are in the eye and nose of the deer. 2-1/8" x 1-1/4". $25-40.

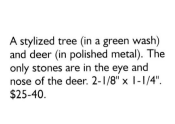

A green enameled tree with a red star and pot. The textured gold edge of the tree also creates its garland. Small colored stones (6) sparkle like balls on all three tiers. 2-3/16" x 1-1/2". $35-50.

This tree is built by using five tiers of loops with tiny gold balls. Each loop has a pastel stone (15) with four smaller stones hanging off the bottom. 2-3/8" x 1-1/2". $35-50.

This tree is commonly referred to as the "Banana Tree." Four tiers of banana branches swoop upward with multi-colored stones (10) sitting above each one. 2-1/4" x 1-1/2". $35-55.

This tree is also built by using five tiers of loops and tiny blue balls. Each loop has a pastel stone (15) with four smaller stones hanging off the bottom. 2-3/8" x 1-1/2". $35-50.

A tree whose edges are like prickly pine needles. The inside of the tree is divided into sections with jewel tone stones (11). 2-1/2" x 1-1/8". $35-45.

One tree is in antique metal and the other is in a green enamel. 2-1/4" x 1-1/2". $35-55.

A comical Santa tree. The star and Santa's hat tassel are created from holly flowers and leaves. 2-3/8" x 1-3/4". $35-55.

A gold tone tree similar to another tree designed by Beatrix. This tree uses colored stones while the other tree uses enamel. 2-1/2" x 1-5/8". $25-35.

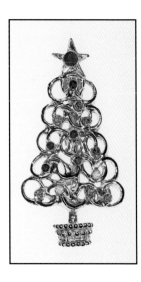

A silver tree created by overlapping circles. Tiny colored stones are sprinkled over it. 2-3/8" x 1-1/4". $35-45.

B.J.
1975 ~ 1983

The Beatrix mark was used until the company was sold to Treasure Master in 1975. It then changed the mark to "B.J.", meaning "Beatrix's Jewels." B.J. went out of business in 1983.

An open tree with two red swinging bells and tiny green stones (6). 2-3/8" x 1-5/8". $35-45.

A very simple brushed green enameled tree. It has just five sets on its branches plus a red set in the star. 2-1/8" x 1-1/2". $25-40.

This tree is made of half tiers in gold tone with red and white enameled candy canes. 2-1/2" x 1-5/8". $25-35.

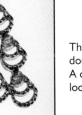

The tree was created by double loops of beaded rope. A clear stone sits atop each loop. 2-3/8" x 1-5/8". $35-55.

A simple tree whose center is decorated with red (6), green (11), and clear (2) stones. Gold tone balls are also used. 2" x 1-1/2". $25-35.

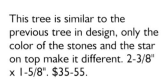

This tree is similar to the previous tree in design, only the color of the stones and the star on top make it different. 2-3/8" x 1-5/8". $35-55.

A tree enameled with a silver blue color. It has five tiers with molded clear balls. 2-3/16" x 1-1/2". $25-35.

Here is the traditional tree shape. The balls hanging on the tree are little colored stones (12). 1-3/4" x 1-1/2". $45-95.

An arrow-shaped tree filled with stones (10) of traditional Christmas colors. The top and bottom are balanced with a single stone. 1-1/2" x 1". $30-45.

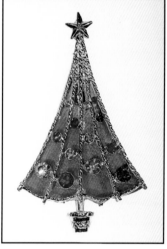

The tree is gold tone with an open back, and has (13) colored sets in graduated sizes. 2-3/8" x 1-5/8". $35-50.

This tree is silver with a green enamel background, and has (13) color sets in graduated sizes. 2-3/8" x 1-5/8". $35-50.

A brushed gold tree with six multi-colored candles and a red stone in the star. 2-1/4" x 1-1/2". $20-40.

Little green stones (8) surrounded by green enamel creates a tree with very interesting texture. 1-3/8" x 1-1/4". $45-95.

A brushed gold body with concave colored balls. Same design was seen earlier with colored stones. 2-1/2" x 1-3/4". $20-40.

A flat narrow tree in a "stain glass" design of red, green, and blue. One red stone sits on the trunk. 2-3/4" x 1-1/4". $40-55.

A green washed tree with recessed ornaments using washes. 2-1/2" x 1-3/4". $25-35.

Three variations of a tree in a sleigh. There are tiny enameled balls on each tier of the tree. The tree's star has a single stone in it's center. 2" x 1-1/4". $35-45.

Here are four diagonal tiers in a blue wash. The garland uses blue and clear stones (26). 2-1/4" x 1-1/4". $35-50.

A flat cone shaped tree designed with star shaped stones (6) set inside larger cut out stars. 2-1/2" x 1-7/8". $40-60.

A simple gold tree in three layers. A single stone sits in each section of the tier. 2-1/8" x 2". $20-35.

A tree whose left side is concave and right side is convex. 2-1/2" x 1-1/2". $40-60.

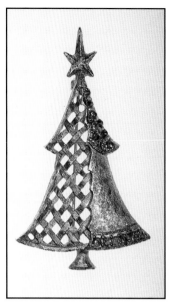

A marcasite tree of cutout, overlapping branches. 1-1/8" x 1-7/8". $35-55.

A small green enameled tree with one red stone in it's star. 2" x 1". $25-35.

An unusual and hard to find silver tree. Left side is a basket weave with the right side a brushed silver. Blue stones sit on the right top branch with pink stones on the bottom right. 2-1/2" x 1-1/2". $100-125.

A tree with green enamel petals and colored stones (15). 2-3/8" x 1-3/4". $40-55.

Three layers of "bells" stacked on top of each other. A red and white garland crisscrosses over all the tiers. 1-1/4" x 2". $25-35.

This tree comes in a bright gold and in an antique gold finish. It has seven jagged edged tiers set with tiny stones (11) in raised stars. 2-3/4" x 1-1/4". $35-55.

One side is concave and one is convex. It is brushed silver with light pink sets (8). This tree and the Giovanni are very similar in design. 2-5/8" x 1-5/8". $50-65.

Similar designs, but one hangs on a chain from "Merry Christmas" in red enamel. Both trees are covered with red and white candy canes and ornaments. Musical. Hanger: 2-5/8" x 1-1/4". $25-55. Pin: 2-1/2" x 1-5/8". $40-55.

This tree has many prickly green enamel branches which swoop downward with sparkling balls (15). It has a red enamel pot. 2-1/4" x 1-3/4". $35-55.

Shiny metal with ice colored pastel stones. 2-1/2" x 2-1/2". $50-65.

Belle Originals

This is a rough copy of the previous Bellini trees with the metal in a rough silver. Stone shapes and arrangement are the same except for only one stone in the pot. 2-1/2" x 2-1/2". $40-55.

This tree was designed by Belle Originals. The design looks much like the Hagler designs with it's beading, large star, and elaborate backing. Not as well made as the Hagler, but still interesting. 2001. 4" x 2-1/4". $85-150.

Benedikt N.Y.
1950 ~ ?

Although no longer in business, Benedikt jewelry is highly collectible and sought after.

Bellini
1922~ 2002

Two trees by Bellini. The style and stone arrangement is exactly the same, only the color of the stones differ. In the first, the metal is black with dark colored stones. The stones are of all sizes and shapes. This tree is unique due to the combination and arrangement. 2-1/2" x 2-1/2". $50-65.

Gold tone trees which are molded in five tiers with one tree using red and green stones and the other using all green stones for ornaments. 2" x 1-3/4". $35-45 each.

A gold tone tree molded in five tiers with red and green rhinestone ornaments (23). It was also made with red and clear rhinestones. The pot is set with clear rhinestones (17). This tree can be found marked and unmarked. 2" x 1-3/4". $35-55.

A squashy layered tree with slightly textured branches. It uses green, red, and clear stones (7). Four gold balls dangle from the tree. 1-3/8" x 1-1/2". $55-75.

Here a small, squat, convex tree is decked with glass balls (9) in red and green. 1-1/2" x 1-1/4". $75-90.

Les Bernard
1963 ~ 1970s

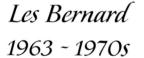

The Les Bernard Company was founded in 1963 by Lester Joy and Bernard Shapiro, the son of Harold Shapiro who, with two other partners, founded Vogue in 1936. Thus the name of Les Bernard was created. *(Ball & Torem, 1996.)*

Two cute little trees which have layered branches. The tips of these branches are decorated with jewel tone stones (6) with three more going down the center of the tree. The star and trunk are solid metal. These pins might have been scatter pins or a sweater guard set which was popular in the 1960s. 1-1/8" x 1". Set: $25-35.

B G
2000 ~ 2002

Bee Gee McBride

Collage Technique

Bee Gee McBride was born and raised in Texas. She has a diverse background in and out of the field of design. She has studied fashion design, art, and design. She has also taught painting and is a lecturer on antique jewelry and accessories and a showwoman for her vintage jewelry. She ran her first antiques shop in the 1980s and early 1990s. A new store was opened in 1996 where she has concentrated on collecting and selling vintage jewelry, accessories, and linens. She developed her internet web site and store in 1997. In the summer of 2000, Bee Gee started designing and creating Christmas tree pins. Thus, she developed her Christmas Tree Forest, which is a specific feature of her South Texas Trading Company.

Bee Gee McBride uses both vintage tree bases as well as ones she has designed herself. Then she applies antique glaze, followed by her "collage" technique using faceted, pronged, and crystal stones. Each one is one-of-a-kind. Here is how Bee Gee explains *collage*: "An artist chooses collage techniques to capture color, shapes, and texture. By creating a design with shapes, texture, and color, a two-dimensional surface is created that gives the eye several places to rest and gives the piece movement. I like to see collage in jewelry because it enables me to use wonderful shapes and colors of stone without worrying about perfect mountings and settings. I *make* the settings as I have done on my headlight trees with Swarovski chains forming a ring around the large 20 mm stones. A collage tree will last every bit as long as a bench-made piece designed with a torch and solder."

An interesting tree with golden pears alternating with clear rhinestones. Clear baguettes create a garland between each tier. 2000. 2-3/4" x -1-1/2". $45-55.

A Christmas tree made to show the Spirit of America after the tragedy of September 11, 2001 in New York City. 2-1/2" x 1-3/4.". $35-45.

The "Snow Tree" looks like it just snowed. Decorated with clear snow balls and light blue baguettes. 2000. 2-1/2" x 1-1/2". $30-40.

"Nancy's Pink and Purple Tree." It was named and designed for the author with the combination of purple stones down the middle and pink flowers on the edges. 2000. 2-1/4" x 1-7/8". $35-45.

Collage design.

This is one of the "headlight" series of pins. Each green stone (6) is outlined in clear rhinestones. Tiny green sets in the pot really sparkles. 2000. 2-1/2" x 1-5/8". $45-55.

Another tree (from the headlight group) in a different style. Large red stones dominate this tree with clear rhinestones on the edges. There are two baguettes down the center. 2000. 2-1/8" x 1-1/2". $45-55.

A "Fruit Salad" pin of red flowers (15) with clear rhinestone centers and green leaves at the bottom edge. 2000. 2-3/4" x 2-1/2". $40-55.

Glass opalescent flowers set with a gold pin. 2000. 2-1/4" x 1-3/4". $35-45.

Two trees using the same style form which feature snowballs. One uses milkglass balls with pink and green stones, while the other uses an aurora borealis milk glass set with pink and aurora borealis stones. 2000. 2-1/8" x 1-1/2". $25-35. 2-1/8" x 1-1/2". $25-40.

B.N.
2000 ~ 2002

Barbara Newman

Barbara Newman is an artisan whose first passion is jewelry making. She has been involved with jewelry design for over 20 years. Her unique glass design captures the mystical qualities of glass in bold colors and textures. Each piece is unique. There are never duplicates. Barbara's glass design also reflect holistic elements of body, mind and spirit by combining color, shape, and dimension with times of spirituality. Those who admire her work say that she has the unique ability to capture a spiritual essence in her work. There is a zen-like quality for her contemporary designs. Barbara's has studied all over the United States with premier glass artists. She is a registered pharmacist with a holistic certification.

These designs are cut by hand and then fired in a kiln. They are made of a combination of fusible and dichroic glass. 2001.

"Blue Spruce" tree tipped with gold. 2-3/4" x 1-3/4". $35-55.

Tree with wire and glass beads. 3-1/2"x2-1/4". $35-65.

Tree upon tree. 2-5/8"x1-1/2". $35-65.

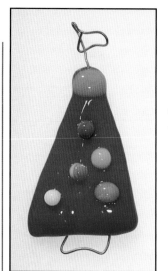

Tree with glass beads and wire topper. 3" x 1-1/4". $35-55.

Bijoux-STERN
1960s ~ 2002

A beautiful French piece by Bijoux-STERN. Three tiers of heavy green enameling are outlined in tiny rhinestones. Different sizes and shapes of stones decorate the tree. Below the tree are several packages set-off in red and blue enamel. Came in its original marked cloth pouch. Sent from London. 1990s. Unmarked. Bijoux-STERN made very few Christmas pins. 3" x 1-15/16". $75-125.

Bonetto ®

DIGITS™ by Bonetto ®

Design for DIGITS™. A unique wire tree strung with glass beads, stars, and a watch with rhinestones. Watch made in Japan. 3-1/8" x 2-1/4". $50-75.

Marcel Boucher
1937 ~ 1971

Marcel Boucher founded his company in 1937. His jewelry showed great creativity and had great quality. Most of the jewelry is marked and carries an inventory number.

This tree features two layers with many cut-out tiers. Tiny glass and opaque stones (24) are sprinkled over the tree. Note the detail of the roots. Mark: Marcel Boucher or Boucher. 2-1/4" x 1-1/2". $75-125.

Gay Boyer

An open design with gold balls. The center is a ball of enamel in red, green, and blue. A pretty green enamel bow sets off the bottom of the tree. 2001. 2-1/4" x 1-1/2". $10-15.

Brooks
1960s ~ 1970s

This tree is also in the "harp" style. Pronged. 2-1/2" x 2". $45-65.

This tree is known as the "Harp" due to its cast wires that move from the center upward to each limb. Pronged. 2-1/4" x 1-3/4". $40-55 each.

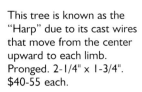

This tree has open branches with the bottom layer in unpolished metal while the top layer is shiny. Baguette rhinestones (12) form the trunk. The branches have small multi-colored stones hanging from their tips. Pronged. 2-1/2" x 2". $35-55.

The tree is the same design as the previous tree, but uses only clear rhinestones (12). Pronged. 2-1/4" x 1-1/4". $40-50.

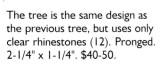

Butler & Wilson
1968 ~ 2000

Two British designers, Nicki Butler and Simon Wilson, began their careers as jewelry dealers in the late 1960s. Their interest was in the Art Nouveau and Art Deco periods. In 1980 they started expanding their business in London, to the U.S.A. and Glasgow. The inspiration for many of their new creations has come from favorite old pieces in their own collections. Realizing a market for modern versions of their originals, they began to copy and rework their "old favorites" into new pieces. (*Becker, 1991*)

A wonderful glitzy pin by the British design house Butler and Wilson. There are many multi-colored crystals in different sizes and shapes on gun-metal plating. There are nine baguette candles with gold flames. Pronged. 1990's design. 4-1/4"x2-5/8". $200-275.

This tree has pearls (10), navettes (25) in red, green, and clear with round stones of two sizes (18). Pronged. 3-1/4" x 2". $195-250.

The outline is in emerald green stones, while the body is filled with pinks, lavenders, citrines, and clear rhinestones. 1-1/8" x 1-3/4". $125-150.

This is the same style as the old classic red, blue and clear stones shown in this section. Designed with pears and rounds, this is an exciting looking piece. As always, the quality is great. Also nestled in this pin are ten clear candles with flames. This pin in both colors makes a real statement when worn. 3-1/4" x 2-1/16". $195-250.

All gold pin with accents just on the snowman's face and buttons (5). 1-3/4" x 1". $35-45.

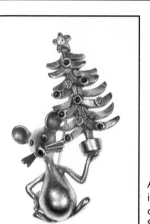

A cute little mouse balancing a tree on its palm. Red and green stones (13) on mouse and tree. 2-1/4" x 1-3/4". $35-45.

BW

This tree is signed BW but it is *not* a Butler & Wilson. Butler & Wilson always has an ampersand (&) between the two letters, "B&W."

Here angels (11) are stacked in four tiers. Each angel has a pearl crystal body and a pearl head. The trunk and tree top is also an angels. 2-1/2" x 1-1/2". $55-75.

Cadoro
1955 - 1980s

A stacked angel tree. Each angel has its arm extended outward holding onto a star with a rhinestone. 2-3/4" x 2-3/16". $65-85.

A cute little tree which is highly textured in gold tone. Little dangling glass balls (10) decorate the body. The pin itself is not marked, but the pin came in a box marked "by Capri." 2-3/8" x 1-3/8". $20-30.

Capri
1954 - 2002

Ads for Capri date back as far as 1954 in *Glamour* magazine and 1965 in *Vogue* magazine. (Stringham, 1999)

A very glitzy tree on a silver backing. It is made up of chatons and navettes in different colors. Pronged. 2-7/8" x 1-1/2". $45-60.

An older tree whose limbs are layered. Each limb is deeply textured. There are green and white baguette candles (6), with no flame. There are dark blue and clear stones scattered over the tree. 1-7/8" x 1-1/2". $65-75.

Hattie Carnegie
1918 - 1970s

  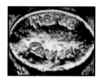

Hattie Carnegie started out in the retail apparel business and later created jewelry to accessorize her clothing.

Here are four jagged tiers sprinkled with rhinestone edges. Multi-colored navettes (12) sit nestled in the tiers. The star and pot are adorned with clear rhinestones. Marked and unmarked. 2-1/2" x 1-3/4". $60-125.

A prickly edged tree whose branches stand out at different angles for a three-dimensional effect. It is green enameled with a multi-color rhinestone garland hung loosely over the tree. 2-3/8" x 1-1/2". $150-195.

This tree has rhinestone loops decorated with different colored pear and navette stones. Ever so often a lacy green branch sticks out from under a loop. Marked and unmarked. 2-1/2" x 1-1/2". $85-160.

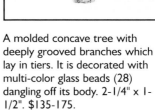

A molded concave tree with deeply grooved branches which lay in tiers. It is decorated with multi-color glass beads (28) dangling off its body. 2-1/4" x 1-1/2". $135-175.

This tree is a stacked diamond design. The gold frame is notched and each rhinestones (36) looks like it has been individually attached to the next rhinestone. It is delicate with real sparkle. 2-1/4" x 1-3/8". $135-175.

Carolee

1978 ~ 2002

Carolee Friedlander founded Carolee Designs in 1972. Christmas pins were first issued in 1987. She has created several Christmas tree pins.

Wonderful light-up trees which are the same except one has a blue stone base. The trees are cone shaped with rows of colored stones. Battery is set in the base. 2-1/2" x 1-3/8". $70-125 each.

This is a wonderful three-dimensional design tree. The branches project outward on three sides and are flat on back. The glass baubles are red, blue, white and green. 1-7/8" x 1-1/2". $80-120.

This Carolee tree is a stacked diamond design in eight rows. Each diamond shape is filled with colored stones. 2-1/4" x 1-1/2". $135-175.

A Carolee tree in textured gold with a tiny rhinestone garland. Each point has a colored stone (6) set in a star motif. Numerous other stones (20) decorate the tree. It was purchased on a black card in 1999. 2 " x 1-5/8 ". $45-60.

Castlecliff
1938 ~ 1977

Castlecliff, Inc. was founded by Clifford Furst in New York City in 1938. Its designs used plated metals, enamels, and beads.

The little Christmas tree angel is made with snappy red and green enamel. The arms and legs are a twisted gold metal rope. In each hand is a white enamel candle with a red flame. Charming. 1-7/8" x 1-3/4". $45-55.

This tree uses the same exact enamel colors of red, green and white as used in the previous tree. The same candle design also is used on three tiers underlined by the same rope design. This is an interesting variation of the above tree. 2" x 1-3/4". $55-65.

Catalano
1985 ~ 2002

John L. Catalano literally grew up learning about jewelry making at his grandfather's knee. His grandfather was a master jewelry maker of fine jewelry. In his house he had a small shop where he could "catch up" on work he had taken home from his jewelry shop. It was there, between the ages of six and eight, that John "fiddled around" learning about what jewelry

John L. Catalano

making was all about. Even at this early age, his grandfather saw that John had potential and taught him how "to do things the right way." He learned how to file pennies until the face was gone, how to drill a hole in the penny and then set a stone and raise it. John later moved in with his grandfather and continued his learning about repairing.

His restoration career came first. He was a diamond setter and bench jeweler of fine jewelry. People were always bringing jewelry in to be fixed. At one time, Catalano owned his own jewelry store. He closed it and set up at a flea marked to liquidate his jewelry. One of the dealers at the show asked him if he cold fix several broken designer pieces for her. When he brought back the pieces repaired, she asked him if he had really done this work himself. The work was so good she told him that an occupation in repair could be very lucrative for him. So Catalano took the instruments and tools he used for fine jewelry making and made the modifications needed to work on costume jewelry. Due to his technique and skill, he says, "my restoration abilities and skills have changed how people buy antique costume jewelry throughout North America. Even though a wonderful piece of old jewelry is broken, with great restoration work more pieces are being bought for repair and resale. Thus the dealer can turn around and sell it and make money." One of his customers told him that he had become the "Harry Winston of costume jewelry." He is the official authorized restoration person for the Eisenberg Jewelry Company.

Catalano became interested in costume jewelry design when he discovered he could mimic antique jewelry even though he was creating a brand new piece. He considers himself an underground designer. No mass production. All work from beginning to end (platting to signature) is done by him. He started designing costume jewelry of all kinds, including Christmas trees, when people came to him and asked him to design a specific piece for them. He creates jewelry with an attitude. His jewelry is for "the self confident." His first piece of costume jewelry was an eyeball crying blue topaz stones. The sky is the limit for Catalano whether he is making crowns, Mardi Gras

This tree was made especially for me. It is made of navettes and rounds in emerald green, ruby red, and fuchsia. There are several clear squares down the center of the tree with one on the tree's top. Blue ovals are layered on top of the bottom layer. Two garlands are swagged across the tree: one in rhinestone, and, one in a gold chain. Hanging from the rhinestone garland are red and light green glass balls. Pronged. 2001. 4-1/2" x 2-1/2". $300-500.

masks, jewelry for the stars, or whatever. Currently some of his pins can be seen on album covers and in magazine articles by The Bongiovi Entertainment Group. Jewelry restoration and creation are one part of his life. He is also a published writer and songwriter.

This tree was made for Kathy Flood. Here the tree, as well as the garland, is made of clear, round rhinestones. Navettes in red, green, and blue fill the inside of the tree. Clear rhinestones create the tree's spine from the top navette down to the pot. Dark red and light green glass balls hang down from the garland. Pronged. 2000. 4-3/8" x 3-1/8". $300-500.

New tree with multi-colored stones (19) in three sizes. A halo adorns the top stones. 2000. 3-3/8x1-3/4". $35-45.

Alice Caviness
1945 ~ 1983

A new tree designed in half red rhinestones and the other half in green. Marks: Celebrity N.Y., Celebrity. 2-5/8" x 1-3/8". $30-45.

An open tree of textured gold. Multi-colored stones are set in between the vertical branches (9). Very hard to find. 2-1/2" x 1-3/8". $55-85.

A tree with a tiny bead design on its outer edge. It is decorated with unusual shaped pockets of green enamel and tiny pastel rhinestones (12). A metal ball tops the tree. 2-3/8" x 1-1/2". $40-50.

Celebrity N.Y.

Celebrity is thought to have been sold through a home party plan similar to Emmons and Sarah Coventry.

Cerrito

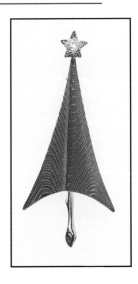

A convex tree in green textured enamel. A gold star with clear stone dons the top. 1-1/4" x 1-3/8". $55-65.

Cini
1920s ~ 1970 and 1993~

Guglielmo Cini was the jewelry artist who founded his company in 1922. It ceased operations in 1970, but started again in 1993. Cini died in 1979. (*Rezazadeh, 1998*)

A beautiful gold tree with silver balls. The tree is unmarked but came in an original box marked Claiborne. 2000. 2-1/4" x 1-1/4". $25-35.

A beautiful sterling silver tree. There are dangling golden balls (10) hanging off little projectile branches. Marked Sterling and Cini. 2-1/4" x 1-3/8" $75-110.

A modernistic silver and gold tree. 1966. 1-7/8" x 1-3/8". $40-55.

Liz Claiborne
1955 ~ 2002

This tree is created from green glass. It is decorated with metal balls and rhinestones. 1966. 2" x 1-3/4". $40-55.

Outline design with rhinestone balls in the branches (7). 1999. 1-1/2" x 1-1/4". $20-35.

Outline design with a trunk line of rhinestones (10). 1999. $20-35.

A gold tone tree with a scroll design on it. There are multi-colored stones (17) scattered over the three tiers. 1966. 1-7/8" x 1-3/8". $40-55.

A unique and fanciful tree. The tree itself has golden tiers with a lamb's head as it's topper. A sprig of holly leaves tops off the lamb's hat. All decoration is enamel. 1-7/8" x 1-1/4". $25-35.

A little silver tree set with silver balls, stars, and tiny red, green, and blue stones. This design is similar to an old JJ design. Sold under the name "Villager" which is a division of Liz Claiborne. 1999. 2-1/8" x 1-3/4". $15-25.

A brushed gold tree with a wavy garland of pave' rhinestones. 1999. 2-1/8" x 1-5/8". $25-35.

Lindsay Claire Designs

A silver tree in four tiers with scalloped edges and red, green and clear stones stones (9). 2 -3/8" x 1-3/8". $30-45.

A beautiful pewter tree with candy canes, an angel and a package hanging from the bottom of the tree. The tree is designed with garlands, bows and a star on top. 2000. 2-1/4" x 1-5/8". $40-50.

Corel

Corel is a division of Coro.

A wonderful tree with great movement in its branches. Much open work gives it an airy, but elegant feeling. A combination of red, blue and green stones (13) decorate this tree with several groupings of clear rhinestones in the middle. A very eye catching design. 1-7/8" x 1-3/8". $40-65.

A slightly concave tree, in green enamel, which is etched and slightly open between each tier. Colored rhinestones decorate the bottom branch while clear rhinestones decorate the pot. 2 -3/8" x 1-1/2". $45-60.

Five scalloped tiers set with two sizes of red, green, and clear stones The tree is a brushed gold with a beaded edge. It is open between each tier. 2 -7/8" x 1-7/8". $35-55.

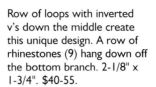

Row of loops with inverted v's down the middle create this unique design. A row of rhinestones (9) hang down off the bottom branch. 2-1/8" x 1-3/4". $40-55.

Coro
1919 - 1979

Coro dates back to 1901, but didn't use the name Coro until 1919. It was in business until 1979. Coro started a holiday division called Mylu in 1968. Coro had other divisions such as Corocraft, Corel, and Vendome.

A bright green wash covers this very abstract looking tree. Eight tiny stones sit in a star cut design. 2-1/4" x 2-1/8". $40-50.

Here leaves in a green wash have a garland of red and clear stones (21). 2-1/4" x 1-3/8". $45-55.

Unmarked tree of brushed silver in four tiers. Each tiers has colored stones (11). A double star with a rhine-stone sits on the top. 2-1/2" x 1-1/4". $35-45.

A beautiful gold looped tree with three longer tiers on the right side and four shorter tiers on the left. The edges are a ribbon of polished metal. 2 1/8" x 1 7/8". $40-55.

Tree of brushed gold with red and green stones.Marked. 2-1/2" x 1-1/4". $65-75.

Corocraft
1937 ~ 1979

Corocraft was a division of Coro started in 1937.

An open-cut diamond design with a twisted tree trunk. Marked: PAT PEND. COROCRAFT. 2-1/2" x 1-1/2". $35-60.

A light-up cone tree in brushed gold with a dozen multi-colored sets alternating in rows of twos and threes. It uses a battery. Probably the 1960s. 2-1/8" x 1-1/4". $100-140.

Sarah Coventry
1949 ~ 1984

A tiny tot lapel pin. It has two enameled tiers with a red enamel garland. On top is a gold star with a single rhinestone. 1-1/8" x 1/2". $15-30.

The tree has a textured silver finish with green (14) and red (14) stones. A star with a red stone sits on top. 2-3/8" x 1-3/8". $25-35.

Cristobal
1985 ~ 2002

Steven Miners and Yai of Cristobal, 26 Church Street, London

"The greatest pleasure for us is finding collectors that appreciate our pieces and wear them. We delight in tales of ladies going to social events and receiving rave comments from their friends. It makes it all worthwhile."

Steven Miners started Cristobal in a small stall at the bottom end of London's Portobello market in 1985. This happened after a lucky find of a Christian Dior set he bought for the equivalent of $25. Having just gotten out of the Army, and with no background, he found that this was a great way to pay his bills. Since much jewelry in Europe was misunderstood and much under valued, there was money to be made in buying and reselling. That was the heyday of beautiful jewelry which was affordable. Cristobal (whose name was inspired from the word crystal and Balenciaga) has always concentrated on reselling. Although the emphasis has been on buying costume jewelry, the shop also handles compacts, and handbags. In 1988 Cristobal relocated to Alfies Antique Market. In 2002, it moved to 26 Church Street. The shop specializes in costume jewelry of the 1920's to the present from dealers all over the globe. In 1993 Yai joined the business and the company expanded it's sales on the Internet and mail orders. It was this new energy which was behind the desire to create and sell jewelry created by themselves. This innovation started in 1997. It took two years to find manufacturers to do the labour intensive work and to find a source of vintage stones. This project finely took-off in early 1999. The first collection was a limited to 16 butterflies in four colors. Following the butterflies, there were six Christmas tree pins. Both the butterflies and the Christmas trees were a much greater success than either Steven or Yai expected. There have been a number of additional pins created since then. Cristobal's mission continues to be to create something of value, collectability, and individuality which Steven and Yai believe their customers deserve. As for the future, they plan to keep on producing more Christmas trees along with other themes including bug pins, flowers and large stunning necklaces in both bib and choker designs. It is important to them that the quality remain high and the design be individualistic. Wherever possible, old stones will be used in their pieces to maintain the quality they desire. Plating will be mostly Palladium or Gunmetal with all stones hand-set and hand soldered. Some pieces will be issued as "Limited Edition," but many will be issued at a maximum of 50 pieces depending upon the availability of stones. All pieces will come with certificates of authenticity. *Used with permission from Cristobal.*

This tree has green stone branches with multi-colored stones hanging down between each one. A gold bow ties it together at the trunk like a bouquet of flowers. Gun metal back. Pronged. New 1999. 2-3/4" x 2-1/2". $65-85.

A crystal deco hexagon tree. Inspired from a deco design from the 1920s-1930s. It has crystals, ruby cabachons, and green baguettes on a rhodium plated finish. 3-1/2" x 4-1/2". $275-325.

A tree of vibrant rose navettes. They are offset by the stunning contrast of clear rhinestones. Pronged. Rhodium plated. 2001. 2-1/2" x 4". $75-125.

A wonderful tree with a large variety of different sizes and colors of stones. It is accented with pearls. Gun metal back. Pronged. 4-1/8" x 2-1/2". $145-195.

Lava stones! These pieces look like chunks of lava, but in colored glass. Between the rectangular pieces are ruby red chatons (4). The pot is the same red stones (25). A clear pear-shape stone is on top and two clear stones are the trunk. Only ten trees were made. 1999. 4-1/8" x 2-1/4". $145-195.

A candle tree in green crystal stones with bright red balls. It has three clear baguette candles and a pear on top. Gun metal back. Pronged. 3-1/2" x 1-1/4". $85-125.

A large glitzy tree in emerald green stones. It is decorated with multi-colored stones of different sizes. Goldplated backing. Pronged. 4-3/8" x 3". $185-225.

Danecraft
1939 ~ 1977 ~ 2002

Founded as the Primavera Brothers Jewelry Company in 1939, the brother of the founder renamed the company Danecraft, Inc. In 1977 the name was changed again to the Felch-Wehr Co. All these trees were sold new for $10 at J.C. Penny stores. Mark: Danecraft and St. Nicholas Square. These marks are still in use today.

A silver tree with gold balls. 1999. 2-1/8" x 1-1/8". $15-25.

A gold filigree type tree. 1999. 2-3/8" x 1-3/8". $15-25.

A whimsical pin in eight tiers that wishes you Christmas greetings. 1999. 2-1/4" x 1-1/2". $15-25.

A ribbon tree in red, green, and gold which zigzags itself into seven tiers. 1999. 2-1/8" x 1-3/8". $15-25.

Two identical trees, but one is in green sparkle enamel and the other is in gold tone. Packages dangle off a gold rope. 2-1/4" x 1-1/2". $50-65 each.

A green tree with gold cat. 1999. 1-3/4" x 1-1/2". $15-25.

An open tree with diagonal tiers and a single rhinestone on top. 1999. 2-1/8" x 1-1/2". $15-25.

An enameled cat Santa with a tree. 2-1/8" x 1". $25-35.

DiNicola
1956~1970s

Jerry DiNicola founded his company in 1956. Later it became a part of the Capri jewelry company. The DiNicola mark was not used after the 1970s.

Christian Dior
1947~1957~ 2002

From art dealer to fashion designer, Christian Dior moved into designing jewelry in 1947. In the 1950s, Kramer designed for Dior.

Flat tree of brushed gold. Tiny rhinestones (14) decorate the body. The base has green baguettes (3), red rhinestones (9),with a pot made of green baguette rhinestones (2). 2" x 2". $60-75.

Here is a tailored tree with overlapping textured branches. Each branch has grooved lines running parallel through it. There are ten branches edged in rhinestones. Mark: Chr. Dior. 2" x 1-7/8". $45-60.

Flat tree of brushed gold. This base has all clear baguettes (7) and rhinestones (9). Late 1950s to early 1960s. Mark on raised oval. 2" x 2". $60-75.

Disney

A tree outlined in green stones (42) with a red garland. Mickey heads hang from the garland. 2-1/16" x 1-1/4". $25-40.

Donald Duck, Mickey and Goofy are carrying a tree. This tree was designed for Disney by Napier. 1-1/2" x 2-1/2". $30-45.

This is a Mickey Mouse gold nugget style tree. Red, green, or clear stones create a face and ears. There are a total of four faces using (12) stones in each pin. Quite unique and definitely Disney! 2-5/8" x 1-1/2". $35-45 each.

This is the Blinking Star tree with Donald Duck, Pluto, Mickey, and Goofy who are shown with the tree. 2000. Limited Edition of 1200. 1-7/8" x 1-5/8". $15-25.

This is a light-up enameled tree with Mickey and Minnie standing in front holding a bell and package. 2000. Limited Edition of 1200. 2-1/8" x 1-5/8". $10-15.

Doddz
1952 ~ early 1980s

Doddz tree kits were sold from Jewel Creations in the 1950s-1960s. The frames and stones were sold separately. Consequently, the customer could decorate the tree however he saw fit. Mark: DODDZ.

Dodds, the founder, spelled his name with an "s" at the end, but some of the pins appear to have a "z".

A enameled five piece Mickey Mouse puzzle pin. 1999. 3" x 3". $60-75.

Red and green stones are set down in the metal. Red baguettes (3) down the trunk. 1-1/2" x 1-5/8". $30-40.

Stones are set on top of the pointed branches. 2-1/2" x 1-3/4". $30-40 each.

Dominique
1992 ~ 2002

Dominique pins are made by a man who is very humble and private and does not wish for publicity. He designed for Weiss and Eisenberg Ice. Although he has has been designing for 30 years, he has signed his pieces only since 1992.

A candle tree set with square rhinestones. It has little stones (12) which dangle off its body. 3-7/8" x 2-1/8". $90-125.

A lovely filigree broach with jewels (12) down the middle and along the sides.. A square stone adorns the top. 2-1/2" x 1-1/2". $40-60.

A wonderful color combination of blue (21) and green (6) square stones, accented by a magenta garland of chatons (30), give this piece it's wonderful quality. Pronged. 2-7/8" x 1-1/8". $95-125.

An open triangle set in multi-colored stones (35). This frame is light weight and fragile. 2-1/4" x 1". $20-35.

Here triangular clear crystals (20) are stacked in an open-cut pattern of five tiers. They are topped by a ruby red pear shape. Pronged. 2-1/2" x 1-1/2". $90-125.

An unusual stick pin with three scalloped tiers holding orange stones (6). 1-1/2" x 3/4". $20-35.

Baguettes, pears, navettes, and cabochons in different sizes and colors create the unique quality of this piece. Green accents the base. 3-5/8" x 2-1/4". $90-125.

1999. 3" x 1-3/8". $50-60.

1998. 2-1/2" x 1-15/16". $55-65.

1998. 3-5/8" x 2". $55-65.

Only 11 trees made. 2000. 2-15/16" x 2-3/4". $125-150.

1999. 3-1/8" x 2-3/4". $75-90.

Only 11 trees made. 2000. 2-1/2" x 1-15/16". $60-75.

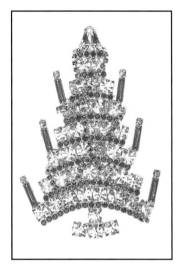

Only 11 trees made. 2000. 3-1/2" x 2-3/8". $125-150. Double signed.

Only 11 trees made. 2000. 3-3/8" x 2-1/4". $60-75.

Beautiful rust-colored glass bead tree with blue and clear accent stones. 1999. 3-1/2" x 2-1/4". $180-250.

Donna Susanne Originals
1993 ~ 2002

Begun in 1993 as Anderson Originals by artist Donna Anderson, this line was started after Donna spent years collecting estate costume jewelry. She worked for a jeweler repairing and soldering broken jewelry, often fixing the unfixable. Donna was inspired by Miriam Haskell jewelry. The tiny bead work and set stones has become a challenge that she enjoys. It is her specialty.

Susanne Travers has been selling antique jewelry for over 25 years and supplies Donna with estate pieces. Together they design a variety of jewelry called Donna Susanne Originals, including beautiful necklaces and broaches from whimsical to elegant, Christmas tree pins, and wire-beaded bracelets. A touch of vintage jewelry is added to each piece making them unique. In July, 2001, the Donna Susanne Originals line was discontinued. The line will once again be marked Anderson Originals.

Here are three pins where glass beads are woven back and forth to create the branches. Colored stones are used for accent. Multi-colored aurora borealis beads cascade across the green glass branches. The tree topper is made of little flowers in the same colors as the garland. Gold bow sits at the bottom. Pronged. 4-1/2'x2-1/2". $180-250.

The star and base are taken from another brass pin. The star holds a red stone. 4-1/2" x 2-1/2". $180-250.

Donna Susanne

Dark navy blue glass beads and clear rhinestones (9) accent this tree. The top and bottom use gold accents taken from another piece of jewelry. 3-3/4" x 2-3/4". $180-250.

Eisenberg
1914 ~ 1970

EISENBERG

In 1880, Jonas Eisenberg started a company in women's fashions. He attached a jeweled accessory to each garment, which was innovative. In 1911 he started his costume jewelry line. In 1930 the jewelry had it's own label attached. A Christmas jewelry line started in the 1950s.

Eisenberg has always had the reputation as being the "best of the best" in jewelry houses. (Ball, 1990, 1997) Although one of the earliest jewelry makers, Eisenberg did not design Christmas pins until the early 1950s. Some of Jonas Eisenberg's jewelry was not marked.

Marks:
Block Letters: 1945-1958
No mark: 1958-1970

Four tree use different colors and one is larger. 2-1/4" x 1-5/8". Trees are identical except for their colors. The tree in the middle with green stones is the only tree marked. 2" x 1-1/2". $50-75 each.

The tree is made of double layers with cut out work between it's branches. The triangular base gives the tree a planted look. Green stones are scattered all over the body of the tree. Boucher designed a tree similar to this one. 2" x 1-7/8". $75-95.

These trees are almost identical except for stone color. Small cabachons (80) are used in a flower design around larger crystals (10). The trees are slightly concave, especially the green. 2-1/4" x 1-1/2". $85-100 each.

The best known and most popular of designs for Eisenberg. It is made with ten loops surrounded by gold balls with a cabachon inside each loop. Rhinestones (19) also decorate the tree. Design first issued in 1972. 2" x 1-1/2". Old versions: $75-125. Newer: $35-50.

This is an early wire tree pin by Eisenberg. The tree was sold with a paper tag. The tree can be seen, with it's tag in the book, *Costume Jewelry* by Fred Rezazadeh. The tree uses red and green stones ((6). It has a hanging base. 2" x 1-1/4". $50-90.

Eisenberg Ice
1935 ~ 2002

Eisenberg Ice was started in 1935 by the Eisenberg company. Maryanne Dolan quotes the story of the family rhinestone business in her book *Collecting Rhinestone and Colored Jewelry* (1990): "Eisenberg Ice evolved when a major department store suggested to my grandfather that he maintain a store facility to satisfy the demand for the rhinestone pins which were being stolen off the Eisenberg Original dresses...This theft became so commonplace Eisenberg took the advice, and the perfect name, Eisenberg Ice, was conjured up by Mr. Karl Eisenberg's father." The scrolled letters mark came first, and the block letters mark was used from 1942.

Marks:
Eisenberg Ice. Scroll letters: 1935- 2002
Eisenberg Ice, Block letters: 1942- 2002

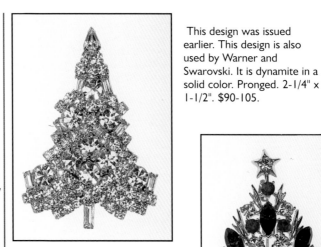

This design was issued earlier. This design is also used by Warner and Swarovski. It is dynamite in a solid color. Pronged. 2-1/4" x 1-1/2". $90-105.

A fragile looking wire style tree set with green navettes (5), red (10) balls, and white (10) balls. Lots of openwork in the design. Pronged. Marked. 1999. 2-3/16" x 1-1/2 ". $45-65.

This elaborate tree is totally covered with tiny emerald green stones. A green pear shape sits on top. There are also three clear rhinestone candles with flames. A loose garland droops off the tree's body. Marked. 1999. 1-5/8" x 1-1/4". $55-65.

These two trees were new in 1999. They came in boxes with the Eisenberg Ice logo. They are smaller than the earlier Eisenberg wire tree pin. Made in gold and silver. 2-1/8" x 1-1/4". $30-40 each.

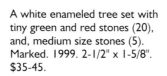

A white enameled tree set with tiny green and red stones (20), and, medium size stones (5). Marked. 1999. 2-1/2" x 1-5/8". $35-45.

A beautiful crystal tree created with two sizes of navettes (16) and chatons (8). The gold prongs add to this tree's beauty. 2-7/8" x 1-7/8". $75-90.

Another version of a tree shown earlier. This tree is smaller, has fewer stones, and the bottom corners of the design are rounded. Marked and unmarked. 1-3/4" x 1-1/4". $25-65.

Each branch of this tree is made up of sparkling dark green crystals. A rhinestone garland (28) drapes loosely off the tree's edges. Different sizes of red (3) and gold (6) chatons complete the design. Pronged. Silver backing. 2 -5/8" x 1-5/8". $65-85.

A simple little tree with a frame of rhinestones. Jewel toned stones decorate the tree (7). Pronged. 1-3/4" x 1-1/4". $55-70.

A reticulated silver tree which is slightly convex. It gives the feelling of marcasite. Decorated all in blue. A different look for Eisenberg Ice. Marked only on its display card. 1999. 2-1/8" x 1-5/8". $50-65.

This tree design is quite exquisite with its five emerald and three ruby candles. The green candles have red flames and the red candles have green flames. Light blue and amber stoness cover the rest of the tree. 2-1/8" x 1-1/2". $65-75.

A textured brushed gold tree with vertical open slits. A rhinestone garland crisscrosses the tree's body. Six aurora borealis balls dazzle between the ropes of rhinestones. Pronged. 2-3/8" x 1-7/8". $85-110.

This design can be seen earlier in the Eisenberg section. These two tiny tots are scatter pins and sometimess can be connected by a tiny chain. Marked on card only. 3/4" x 5/8". $35-45.

Here are six tiers which are cut open between the layers. Tiny beads decorate the edges of the entire tree. Traditional colors of red, green, and clear stones alternate throughout the tree. 2-3/8" x 1-1/2". $35-45.

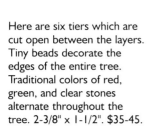

The original design is revisited here in silver. The metal is much lighter than when originally produced. Unfortunately, it is marked only on the original display card. 2" x 1-1/2". $35-50.

A diamond shape tree with pizzazz. This diamond design is textured gold with a recessed tiny emerald chaton (38) in each diamond shape. Red crystals give accent to the tree. A trunk of textured gold braid wraps around the tree's roots. 2-7/8" x 2". $95-125.

This tree looks just like the old white Weiss tree, except it has a molded frame. Tiny gold balls are used along a scalloped bottom edge. Jewel tones in graduated sizes sit recessed in a brushed gold body. Tiny clear rhinestones (17) decorate the scalloped edge, plus, across the entire body. 2-7/8" x 2". $45-65.

A beautiful textured tree with swooping branches adorned with red, green, and gold tear-drops, navettes, and chatons. Rhinestones (27) sparkle atop the tree like snow. Pronged. 2-1/2" x 1-7/8". $85-135.

Lapel pin... Scatter pins... Earrings... Exactly like the earlier Eisenberg tree design. These pins look like they are not marked. When blown up 1600%, the mark became faintly visible on the tree's trunk. The pin cap shown on the shank is not the original one. 1-3/4" x 1-1/4". $35-50.

This tiny tree is created by layered oval-shaped loops. Gold balls and tiny stones (8) create a delicate pin. 1-5/8" x 1-1/4". $35-50.

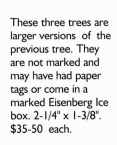

These three trees are larger versions of the previous tree. They are not marked and may have had paper tags or come in a marked Eisenberg Ice box. 2-1/4" x 1-3/8". $35-50 each.

A tree reminiscent of the original Eisenberg tree. This tree however, has "pine cone" balls of dark gold between jewel-tone stones (22). Issued in 1997. 1-7/8" x 1-1/4". $55-70.

These two trees look very much alike. The silver tone is marked, the gold tone is unmarked. This design is created by two rows of diamonds stacked and decorated with tiny balls and chatons. 2" x 1-1/4". $25-35.

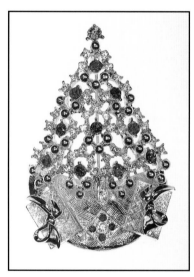

Styled like the original Eisenberg design. It has three small packages at the bottom of the tree. Marked on paper tag only. 2-3/8" x 1-1/2". $80-95.

These two trees are similar in design but one is 1/8" wider than the other. They both have textured branches swooping downward which then turn up holding multi-colored stones. They also use the same number of stones (13) which sit on top of the branches. The second was first issued in 1992. 2" x 1-1/2". and 1-7/8" x 1-3/8". $50-65 each.

This is a newer tree by Eisenberg Ice. There are three tiers which are slightly layered. The edge of each tier is jagged like a real tree would be. A tiny rope garland crisscrosses the tree with jewel tone sets (18). 1-5/8" x 1-1/2". $35-50.

A tree with four tiers of traditional colored stones of red and green (15). Each tier has a raised flower design above the recessed stones. Pot looks like a top hat up-side-down. 2-3/16" x 1-1/2". $45-60.

Oval shaped rhinestone loops, with a red or green navette, create four tiers of branches. The outside of the tree uses tiny red and green stones as balls. The base is all clear rhinestones except for the bottom which is outlined with green stones (9). Pronged. 2-3/8" x 1". $110-125.

A slight variation of a Hollycraft design. This tree however, uses clear rhinestones (30) in the garland with red and green stones (6) on its branches. It is smaller, unmarked and not pronged. 2-1/4" x 1-3/4". $35-50.

Oval shaped loops of emerald green cabachons (8). Each loop has a large clear rhinestone in the middle. The base triangle is filled with ruby cabachons (10). The body is slightly concave. Pronged. Issued in 1950s, again in 1970s and mid 1980s. 2-1/4" x 1-1/2". $70-95.

A necklace tree of green, clear and red chatons. Tree: 3/4" x 5/8". Earrings: 1/2" x 1/2". Per set $35-50.

Five tiers of emerald green navettes (29) set in gold prongs. A red chaton sits in the star on top, and four clear stones create the tree's trunk. Issued in 1996 for $80. 3" x 1-3/4.". $85-120.

A silver tree with silver balls and two sizes of ice blue stones. This is a newer tree (probably the 1970s), although the design is old. 2" x 1-1/2". $55-75.

This design was also used by Warner, and now Swarovski. This same design can also be found unmarked. The tree is made of green crystals, clear cabachon garlands, large colored ornaments, and baguette candles (6). Pronged. First issued in 1992, again in 1998. 2-1/4" x 1-1/2". $90-125.

A simple little green enameled tree decorated with tiny red, blue, and white stones (7). Pronged. 1-7/8" x 1-1/4". $25-40.

A beautifully enameled sleigh holding a tree and a red bow. 1-3/4" x 1-3/8". $30-45.

A wonderful green enameled tree with rhinestones garlands set in gold. 2-1/4" x 1-7/8". $30-45.

Gold lapel pin with red and green rhinestones. 1-1/8" x 7/8". $25-35.

Made with red and green oval shaped rhinestones and four clear round stones. Pronged. 2-3/8" x 1". $110-125.

Emmons
1949 ~ 1980

Charles H. Stuart founded Emmons Jewelers, Inc. in 1949. He used the popular home party plan to distribute the jewelry in the 1950s trough the 1970s. This was the sister company to Sarah Coventry and went out of business in the 1980s.

The Emmons tree is made of round shaped milky white rhinestones, on gold backing with a star on top. The base is a clear rhinestone. Pronged. 2-5/8" x 1-7/8". $110-125.

Eleganté

A simple tree in silver and copper. It is outlined and decorated in goldtone. 1999. 3-3/4" x 2-1/2". $15-25.

A little tailored tree in brushed gold. It is simple but elegant. The bottom edges of the five tiers are slightly raised. Six tiny rhinestones sit recessed in stars. An aurora borealis stone sits on the top star. 1-7/8" x 1-7/8". $45-70.

Fabergé

Fabergé is a Russian jewelry house which was a favorite of the Russian czars for their jeweled eggs.

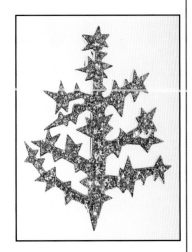

This tree was designed by Fabergé for the Forbes 2000 Christmas Catalog. It is sterling silver set with crystals reminding one of icicles. Mark: Forbes. 2000. 2-1/4" x 1-5/8" $85-100.

This tree has textured gold frame and crisscrossing gold wire. Red, green, and clear stones (8) are scattered over the wires. A flat gold star is at the top. 1998. 3-1/4" x 1-7/8". $30-45.

Fancy That

These silver and gold trees in modernistic designs were purchased in the Hudson Department Store in 1998.

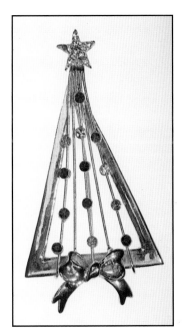

A triangular tree using a curly spider web design. It is decorated with gold stars (6).Marked on card. 1998. 3-1/2" x 1-3/8". $25-40.

Triangular design tree of polished gold wire with a large bow at the bottom edge. Wires run diagonally up from the bottom, with three wires holding the colored stones. The star on top is set with tiny rhinestones. Reissued in 1998. 3-1/2" x 1-3/4". $25-45.

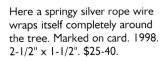

Here a springy silver rope wire wraps itself completely around the tree. Marked on card. 1998. 2-1/2" x 1-1/2". $25-40.

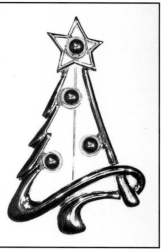

Two trees using a ribbon design. Gold balls on silver tree, while red and clear stones are on the gold. 1998. 2-1/2" x 1-3/4". $25-40 each.

A very tailored tree whose outline is like silver ribbon with parallel lines running through it. A single gold star adorns the top. 1998. 2-1/2" x 1-3/4". $25-40.

The branches are deeply grooved. Small stones in red, green and blue (33) are sprinkled freely over the tree. A larger red aurora borealis stone sits in the star. 2-1/2" x 1-3/4". $75-90.

This is a three dimensional tree with five layers of branches. At the end of the branches are red, green, blue or clear stones (30) in horizontal rows. 2-1/2" x 1-1/4". $95-125.

FO

The FO trees are similar, but mirror images. One is smaller (2-3/8" x 1-1/2") and unmarked while the other is slightly larger (2-1/2" x 1-5/8") and marked. 2000. Marked: $35-45. Unmarked: $15-25.

Florenza
1950s - 1960s

In the 1940s, Dan Kasoff produced this line of jewelry. The "Florenza" mark was probably not used until 1956. (Dolan, 1993)

Here ornate gold loops have a dangling pearl (9) in each loop. A design which can be worn for many different occasions. 3-1/8" x 1-3/4". $45-75.

J.L. Foltz
1997 ~ 2002

J. L. Foltz is a retired man who lives in Columbus, Ohio, where he has worked in Bakelite for five years.

This tree is cut from a flat piece of green bakelite and decorated with different sizes of black Scottie dogs. The middle branches are decorated with black doggie bones. 2000. 2-1/2" x 1-1/16". $105-125.

T. J. Fort

Here is a tree that creates its design from the words "MERRY CHRISTMAS." The letters are cut out and stacked on top of one another. Marked: T. J. Fort. 2-1/16" x 1-3/8". $15-25.

Franklin Mint

Kenneth J. Lane designed this green enamel Christmas tree pin for the Franklin Mint as part of a set. It is cast metal with multi-colored stones of different sizes and shapes and a rhinestone garland. A bow at the bottom is set with a ruby stone. Marked. 2-1/2" x 1-3/4". $50-65.

Gale & Friends
1995 ~ 2002

Gale & Friends has three different lines of Christmas tree pins: marked Gale & Friends, unmarked, and Limited Edition. The tops of the trees are all different and unique. The unsigned pins shown here came from the designer herself.

Here is a bee Christmas tree. The body of this tree has large oval stones in purple, green, and blue. Two busy bees crawl over it. Marked. 4-1/2" x 2-3/4". $65-85.

A fun tree where a red stone garland zigzags horizontally to create the tree's body. A candy cane, a wreath, a star, and several balls hang from the tree's branches below a very ornate topper. Unmarked. 1999. 2-1/16" x 1-3/8". $25-35.

A tree with strands of red stones which end with a gold star. Unmarked. 3-5/8" x 1-1/2". $35-50.

This pin is outlined in sky blue stones. A pink metal rose poses in the middle and again on top. Pronged. Marked. 1999. 4-1/2" x 2-3/4". $40-65.

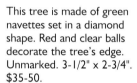

This tree is made of green navettes set in a diamond shape. Red and clear balls decorate the tree's edge. Unmarked. 3-1/2" x 2-3/4". $35-50.

Clear rhinestones create the outline of this tree. The center has four large blue stones and tiny red and green stones. Pronged. Marked. 1999. 4-1/2" x 3-3/4". $45-60.

A Christmas bouquet of flowers having red and green centers. Unmarked. 3" x 1-1/2". $25-35.

Light bulbs set on a bed of rhinestones. Unmarked. 1999. 2-5/8" x 1-7/8". $30-45.

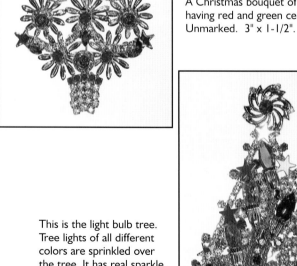

This is the light bulb tree. Tree lights of all different colors are sprinkled over the tree. It has real sparkle. Unmarked. 3-1/4" x 3". $30-40.

An unusual tree with six purple stones enclosed in a gold envelope. Unmarked. 1999. 5-1/4" x 2-1/2". $70-85.

Purple oval stones (7) set in gold loops are stacked on top of one another. A simple gold chain dangles across the tee as a garland. Unmarked. 1999. 3-1/2" x 2-1/2". $50-65.

Navettes (30) abound here in a myriad of colors. A single pear sits on top. Pronged. Marked. 1999. 3-1/2" x 2". $50-65.

A tree made with all green flowers which have a tiny clear center. A gold chain dangles from the tree. Unmarked. 1999. 3-1/8" x 2". $35-45.

Here textured pear stones are stacked in six tiers. A pastel flower sits in the middle. Pronged. Marked. 1999. 3-7/8" x 2". $50-65.

Rows of tiny green stones create this tree. Metal stars and amber stones highlight it. More stones in red and clear fringe the bottom. Unmarked. 1999. 2-3/8" x 2". $35-45.

Jewel tone branches in red, blue, and green are set in gold metal. Candles and stars sit on the edge of many branches. Pronged. Unmarked. 1999. 3" x 2-1/2". $35-45.

An open aurora borealis tree filled with dangling rhinestone chains including an angel. Unmarked. 1999. 4" x 2-1/2". $40-55.

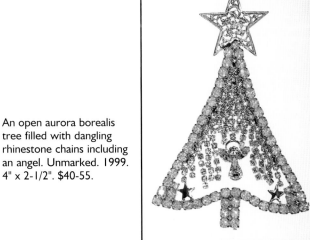

Green jelly ovals stacked together make a dynamic tree. Note the very ornate angel on top. Unmarked. 1999. 3-1/2" x 3". $35-45.

Unusual teal aurora borealis navettes (15) are surrounded by rhinestones. A stunning piece. Pronged. Unmarked. 1999. 3-1/2" x 2-3/4". $60-75.

Carmen Miranda move over! Here is a green navette tree featuring little plastic fruits hanging off its branches. 2000. Marked: Limited Edition. 4-1/4" x 1-5/8". $65-90.

A gold filigree pin in four tiers. There are garlands of gold chain and clear rhinestones. Unmarked. 1999. 3-1/2" x 2-3/4". $35-45.

Here is a wonderful open design with Santa and his sleigh being pulled by Rudolph. 2000. Marked: Limited Edition. 4-15/16" x 3". $85-100.

Lillipops in pastel tones (6) are surrounded by rows of rhinestones. Pronged. Unmarked. 1999. 2-3/4" x 1-3/4". $35-45.

A butterfly tree using clear and pastel stones. Marked. 2000. 3-1/8" x 2". $35-50.

Red and green rhinestone chains are decorated with rhinestone wreaths and a gold metal Scotty dog. Unmarked. 1999. 3-1/8" x 1-3/4". $35-45.

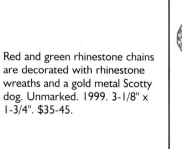

This tree has a single light bulb hanging from each swooping branch. Marked. 2000. 2-3/4" x 2-1/16". $35-50.

Wendy Gell
1975 - 2002

Wendy Gell was president and designer of her own company in New York City and Key West in the 1970s and 1980s. Working as a song writer, she was looking for a way to make a living so she turned to designing jewelry. She invented the "Wristy" cuff bracelet in the '70s and crystal cluster earrings which became immediately popular. Her designs were marketed around the world, worn by movie stars, shown on covers of international magazines, used for "Phantom of the Opera," and Walt Disney Productions ("Roger Rabbit"). She designs a Disney line for Napier and currently sells on the internet. (Gell, 1999)

Germany

A very old tree marked on the back "Made in Germany." It is a molded green tree with painted red balls and an orange star. 2-1/2" x 1-3/4". $20-35.

Gerry's
1950s - 2001

The Christmas tree pin shown above is a one of kind. It uses Swarovski crystals and rhinestones of different shapes on a flat silver base. Her own "gelastic" is used in the background. The green rhinestones are pronged. 3-1/2" x 4". $75-125.

A tree with six tiers of scalloped branches which have a white wash on them. The tiers are connected by tiny painted balls in red, blue, and gold. A green stone sits on the star at the top. 2-1/4" x 1-5/8". $20-35.

This little tree is different from other Gerry designs because it uses layered branches moving downward with tiny colored balls (10). A single pearl sits in the star. 1-7/8" x 1-1/8". $15-20.

This tree has no color, just gold tone with a single clear stone in the star. 1-15/16" x 1-1/2". $15-20.

Similar to the preceding, this tree has space between each scalloped area. It gives a more elaborate look to the tree. 2-3/8" x 1-1/4". $20-35.

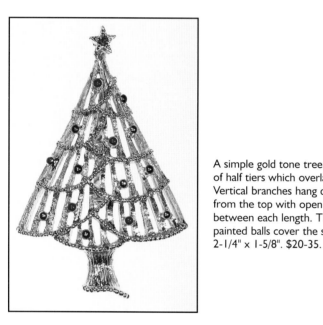

Inverted fans with a red or green ball on each one. 2-1/8" x 1-1/2". $20-35.

A simple gold tone tree made of half tiers which overlap. Vertical branches hang down from the top with open space between each length. Tiny red painted balls cover the surface. 2-1/4" x 1-5/8". $20-35.

There are six tiers of branches in textured gold which are etched with garlands of blue, red, and green. Diagonal branches have open space between them. 2-1/4" x 1-7/8". $20-35.

Similar to those preceding, this tree has three painted balls and three tiny gold balls on each scallop. The bottom scallops and trunk are more sharply curved forward. 2-1/4" x 1-5/8". $20-35.

Two identically styled trees using scalloped limbs with a tiny painted ball on each. The gold tree uses green and gold balls; the silver uses red and green. 1-7/8" x 1-3/8". $20-35 each.

Another similar design with diagonal tiers of tiny leaves and a gold beaded garland which crisscrosses diagonally. 2-1/4" x 1-7/8". $20-35.

A different tree design for Gerry's. The tree is larger and fancier than the other Gerry's designs. The tree's body is green enamel with seven layers outlined in gold. Red balls (13) are scattered over the tree like ornaments hanging down off the branches. 2-1/2" x 2-3/8". $35-50.

A light gold tree using diagonally stroked brush marks. The limbs are open between each tier to give added dimension. No decorations, just plain and simple. 2-1/4" x 1-3/4". $15-25.

These two trees are very similar. However, one is smaller and has a stone in its star; whereas the other has a solid metal star. The branches are looped garlands which make a cut-out design. Tiny painted balls sit between each branch. 1-7/8" x 1-1/4". $20-35.

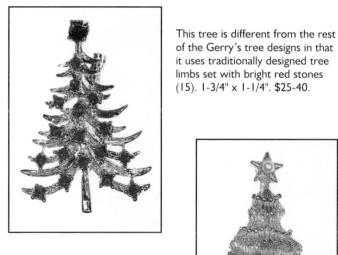

This tree is different from the rest of the Gerry's tree designs in that it uses traditionally designed tree limbs set with bright red stones (15). 1-3/4" x 1-1/4". $25-40.

Here are two nearly identical pins. The right one is a brushed gold with red balls and green washed holly leaves. The left one has red enamel balls with green wash on the tree and a blue wash on the underside of the sleigh. 1-5/8" x 1-1/2". $35-45 each.

A little tree made of four scalloped tiers. A garland of tiny balls decorates each limb. The star on top is set with a pearl. 1-7/8" x 1-1/8". $20-35.

Two trees created by using scalloped branches with tiny painted balls as a garland. The gold tree uses red, blue, and green balls; the silver tree uses blue and green balls. Both have a green stone in its star. 1-7/8" x 1-3/8". $20-35 each.

Gigi / Giusti

A molded tree in green enamel with a tiny rhinestone on top. The angel is in a combination of brushed and polished gold. The angel is wrapping a red enamel ribbon around the tree. Marked: Gigi in script on the tree and Giusti in block letters on the angel. 1-1/4" x 1-3/4". $25-40.

Giovanni

A tailored tree in brushed gold. The triangle shape is creased in the middle. The left side is slightly concave while the right is slightly convex. There are no ornaments, but the tree looks like a rose stem whose bottom has been trimmed at a slant. 2-7/8" x 1-1/4". $50-75.

A set of enamel scatter pins on a card marked Giovanni. Pins have tie-tac backs. Polar bears are decorating a Christmas tree. Set: $10-15.

A set of enamel scatter pins on a card marked Giovanni. Pins have tie-tac backs declare, "I love Christmas trees." Set: $10-15.

Linda Goff

Linda Goff has designed a set of four trees called the "Miracle Beads" Christmas Tree Set. They are made of painted and gilded polymer and are set with "miracle beads." Limited to 100 each. The trees are named: Noel Noir, Indian Pine, White Christmas, and Blue Yule.

Noel Noir. 2000. 2-1/2" x 2". $45 each/set $150.

Indian Pine. 2000. 2-1/2" x 2". $45 each/set $150.

White Christmas. 2000. 2-1/2" x 2". $45 each/set $150.

Blue Yule. 2000. 2-1/2" x 2". $45 each/set $150.

Gold Crown

An open circle design of textured gold in three tiers. The top tier features a point instead of the upper half of a circle. Inside each circle is a red metallic oval (6) with an intaglio star which creates quite a sparkle The tree's base is quite stylized. 2-1/8" x 1". $35-45.

Here is a tree using a textured gold rope design of curved, open circles which are stacked on top of one another in five tiers. It uses metallic ovals of primary colors, plus a silver circle on top. The tree is accessorized with tiny colored stones (6). 2-5/8" x 1-1/2". $35-45.

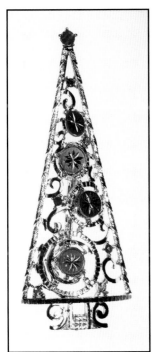

A variation of the two previous pins but made in silver. 3-5/8" x 1-3/8". $35-45.

Another variation of the previous pins but made in silver. 2-1/4" x 1". $25-35.

Walter & Dorothy Goodwich

Walter and Dorothy Goodwich, 28 Dane Street, Kennebunk, Maine. Their mark is printed in gold ink.

A stained glass tree in very dark colors but a high gloss. The quality of work is first class. 1990s. 1-3/4" x 1-1/2". $25-35.

GOP (Grand Old Party)

A gold tone tree sporting a climbing elephant. The elephant has a red stone eye while the tree is decorated with red and green stones (9). The tree's trunk has the letters GOP, for the Grand Old Party (Republican). 1-1/2" x 1-1/8". $35-45.

Gorham

A small tree made in a basket weave design. Multi-colored stones (10) cover the branches. It has a pedestal base. 1-3/8" x 1-1/2". $25-35.

Graziano

Here is a Graziano Christmas tree made of angels and stars on many leafy branches. There are six pearls and five rhinestones stars. At the top the tree is a six-pointed star. 2-3/4" x 2". $75-90.

Rows and rows of ruby red glass petals are layered to create this wonderful tree. The petals are sprinkled with sparkling clear rhinestones (22) for Christmas balls. If you like red, you will fall in love with this tree. 3-1/2" x 1-7/8". $150-235.

Stanley Hagler
1953 ~ 1996

Stanley Hagler, from New York City, made jewelry large and imaginative. His jewelry cannot be mistaken because his designs are unique. He used a specific flower shape in many of his trees, and clusters of simulated seed pearls.

This large tree has a flat back, marquise stones (27), a garland of green Austrian crystals (17), and two crystal rose monteé stars. A large star radiates at the top. 4-1/8" x 3-1/8". $275-350.

This snowy tree has layers of cultured seed pearl leaves. Sparkling ruby and emerald colored stones shine like twinkling lights from behind the pearls. A large rose monteé star radiates at the top. Neither words nor the picture do justice to this pin's beauty. It's my favorite. 3-1/2" x 1-7/8". $275-350.

This is the usual flower theme that Hagler liked to use. Amethyst colored beads are hand wired onto Russian gold-plated filigree. Crystal flower accents with pavé rhinestone teardrops. 2-1/4" x 2-1/4". $175-250.

A different styled flower that uses all dark raspberry and dark green beads. Brighter red and green crystals radiate around the flower's center. The flower on top has a different treatment where the flower is convex with a single stone at the point. 2-1/4" x 2-3/8". $150-225.

A wonderful tree created from seven faux jade leaves. Nine flowers decorate the center in shades of red, pink, and green. Rhinestones are used for accenting the colors. The tree sits in a typical Hagler gold basket. 4-1/8" x 3-1/4". $375-425.

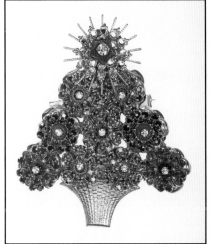

Here are many multi-colored flowers. A large rose monteé star shines at the top of the tree. All stones are prong set on his usual gold plated filigree backing, much like Miriam Haskell's pins. 2-1/2" x 3". $150-225.

A tree of seven large navettes and, in the middle, one large oval stone. The stones are chaton cut. Decorating the tree are five flowers of emerald green and clear rhinestones. A large rose monteé sits on top. Beautiful and bold. 4-1/8" x 3-1/8". $400-450.

A different styled tree than the others. Here the tree is created from individual gold-plated branches wrapped with green glass beads. Four rose flowers go up the center. There are turquoise, pink, red, blue, and clear rhinestones used in this piece. 3-1/8" x 2-1/8". $125-175.

This tree is created from many small leaves arranged like a real flower arrangement. One must turn this tree over and look at the detail work in the metal. The leaves are designed with veins which make the leaves look real. Iridescent stones, which cover the entire tree, reflect the surrounding light. Flowers then add color (red, green, and blue) to the sparkle of the other stones. 3-3/8" x 2-3/4". $250-400.

A fantastic tree with multi-green glass bead branches, a rose monteé, and, ruby red, midnight blue and aurora borealis crystal drops (9). All beads are hand wired onto Russian gold-plated filigree base, A beautiful star using red, green, and aurora borealis stones radiates off the top of the tree. 3" x 2". $350-400.

Here are layered rows of opaque white shaped leaves. Small rose montees' (6) in red and green with alternating middles decorate white milk glass leaves. Crystal dangles in red (2) , green (2), and clear (3) complete the picture. A larger red monteé star rests on top. 3-3/8" x 2-1/4". $175-250.

Here unusual square-cut, aurora borealis stones (28) are used to form this dynamic tree. Pronged. 3-1/2" x 2-3/4". $175-225.

This tree has a green beaded background with crystal angels, stars, and round stones. A gold star is on top. 3-1/2" x 2-1/2". $110-125.

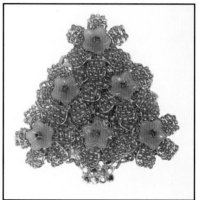

A dynamic little tree created by the typical Hagler flower. Each petal is of deep pink glass stones. Each flower's middle is a lighter shade of pink glass cut into a flower shape. The basket is made from clear rhinestones. 2-3/8" x 2-1/2". $150-200.

A white satin tree in shinny opaque stones. A beautiful pin created out of six large flowers. The center of each flower is a red and green rose monteé. The pot uses the same green stones found in the flowers. 3-1/4" x 2-7/8". $295-350.

Hallmark Cards, Inc.

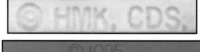

This is one of the most unusual pins in the Hagler collection. I call it the "pineapple and olive" Christmas tree. It can be worn all year round for any occasion, due to the yellow and jet black colors. 2-1/2" x 2-1/2". $85-125.

Here are four Hallmark pins that use a tree as part of its design. They are all molded from plastics.

This sleigh is loaded down with gifts, a tree, and a red bow. 1-1 /2" x 1-3/4". $15-35.

The light-up green tree has a red base and yellow star. Issued 1990. 2-1/2" x 1-1/2". $10-15.

A wonderful tree which just makes one smile. "Jolly Christmas Tree." Original ornament marked 1981. Tree issued in 1982. Hallmark Cards, Inc. 2" x 1-3/8". $25-35.

The rainbow tree is the flattest of the three pins. Although created out of green plastic, this tree has a green sparkle enameled surface. The rainbow and edging are also enameled. Issued 1985. 1-3/4" x 1-3/8". $15-35.

The 1999 pin was inspired by the whimsical Hallmark ornament called "Jolly Christmas Tree." Marked 1999: HMK. CDS. 2" x 1-1/2". $5-10.

The angel has the most depth. She holds a bristle-type tree used in the 1950s. The angel is enameled. Marks: HALLMARK CARDS, INC. HMK. CDS. 1-1/2" x 1-3/8". $15-35.

This 1999 tree has a cute little train that dangles at the bottom. The accompanying Hallmark card declares "A holiday surprise...especially for you from Santa." 2" x 1-1/2". $5-10.

Metal stamped green tree with red balls and a yellow star. 3/4" x 5/8". $15-35.

H in a Heart

This lovely tree has four tiers outlined in polished gold. Red, green, and white stones (41), along with tiny gold balls, enclose each tier. 2-1/4" x 1-1/2". $35-55.

John Handy

John Handy is a contemporary designer.

This cast silver tree has a vertical branch soldered on for a three-dimensional effect. A heavy dot texture is used. Clip-on back. 1990s. Marked twice. 2-5/8" x 1-3/4". $50-75.

HAR

Some feel HAR was associated with Art at one time. Although unmarked, the stone colors are like those used by Art. 1950s.

A wonderful silver tree which is open, layered, convex, and uses different textures. Unmarked. Quality piece. 2-1/4" x 1-3/4". $70-85.

Renata Hart

A little porcelain tree. It has a crackled green finish with tips in gold and dabs of sparkle, 1998. Hand signed: Renata. 1-3/8" x 1-3/8". $25-35.

Haskell

Haskell jewelry is beautifully made. There have never been any Christmas tree pins in the line until 2001. However, founder Miriam Haskell's grandson has recently designed and produced twelve different Christmas trees pins using the Haskell logo.

This tree resembles a beautiful basket of flowers using the Christmas colors of deep red, and emerald green. Clear glass flowers are set with a tiny red stone. Small red dangles hang from the flowers. The back is the typical Haskell backing. 2-1/2" x 2". $125-150.

A stunning rhinestone and gold tree. The branches themselves are set with rhinestones while larger rhinestones dangle off the center of the tree. An eight-pointed star sits on top. 3-3/4" x 2-5/8". $125-150.

Hedy
1960s ~ 1970s

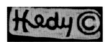

These trees are identical in design but use different colored stones. There are four tiers of wire branches which end in a scalloped edge. Green, orange and amber stones (13) hang from the edge of each tier. 2-1/4" x 1-1/8". $25-45 each.

An enameled tree in a sleigh set with clear and green stones. 2-1/4" x 1-1/8". $25-45.

These three are all the same metal tree using different colored stone combinations. Trees have a diamond design with a tiny ball between each diamond that has a colored stone in it. 2-1/8" x 1-3/8". $25-45 each.

The same trees in different colors, using a flower design. Tiers of flowers with colored stones in the centers create these trees. Tiny gold balls or tiny rhinestones decorate the outside sof the flowers. 2-1/8" x 1-1 /4". $25-45 each.

This gold tree has tiny blue, green, and clear stones (12). 2-1/4" x 1-1/8". $30-40.

HEF

A cute tree in molded plastic made by layering the four branches. All of the decorations sit on top of the tree: star, garland, and balls. Even the packages are dimensional and sit in front of the tree. Dated 1989. Made in Philippines. 3" x 2-1/4". $10-15.

Frances Hirsch

A Hirsch tree with molded branches and tiny red and clear stones (23). The pot has a ring of rhinestones (15). Looks just like the DiNicola trees shown earlier. 2" x 1-1/2". $45-65.

Hobé
1903 ~ 2002

Jacques Hobé started this company in Paris, France, in 1887. He and his son moved it to New York in 1903. The company, now in Mt. Vernon, NewYork, is still run as a family business. Hobé jewelry became known as "Jewels of Legendary Splendor." (Baker, 1986)

Green navettes (13) create each tier of this tree. Each tier is layered to add dimension on a gold backing. Pronged. 2-3/8" x 1-1/2". $145-175

A tree which is designed as a framed picture. The tree is molded on a white background and the frame is pretty and delicate. 2-1/8" x 1-1/2". $65-85.

An early tree with an outline of gold tone metal with a spine and branches of green stones (15) and two amber stones. A red navette on top. Unmarked. Originally sold with paper tag. 1-1/2" x 1/2". $35-50.

Holland Mold

HOLLAND

Ceramic tree in olive glaze. There are seven tiers of individual branches, each with an indentation for a stone. A nice, simple tree. The back is not glazed. 2-1/2" x 2". $20-30.

Rhinestones create the outline of this tree and its crisscrossing branches. Larger red (8) and green (7) stones decorate the tiers. A simple silver star sits on top. Pronged. 2-3/4" x 2". $75-125.

Rhinestones outline this tree and its horizontal tiers. Each tier is layered with rhinestones (14) which dangle freely. Silver backed. Pronged. 2-1/4" x 1-7/8". $115-150.

Similar smaller trees with different glazes and multi-colored stones. The backs are glazed so the marks cannot be seen. $20-30 each.

This white ceramic tree has four tiers of half branches decorated with red stones. 2-3/8" x 1-7/8". $25-35.

The metal around the navette imitates the shape of the candle. The tree itself is created from loops in five tiers with a multi-colored stone at the top of each loop. Unmarked. 2-5/8" x 1-1/2". $75-85.

Hollycraft
1948 ~ 1965

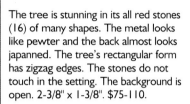

Here is an unusual bare branch tree set with 16 lovely aurora borealis dangling balls. 2-1/2" x 1-7/8". $125-150.

The tree is stunning in its all red stones (16) of many shapes. The metal looks like pewter and the back almost looks japanned. The tree's rectangular form has zigzag edges. The stones do not touch in the setting. The background is open. 2-3/8" x 1-3/8". $75-110.

This is a ribbon tree set in antique gold. It winds back and forth with colored stones (13) set in each curve. The metal looks like real ribbed ribbon. Monet used this design in white. Very hard to find. 2-1/4" x 1-1/2". $225-250.

Pine needle branches are decoratied with six candles and round milky aurora borealis stones. All is in white. This tree comes in several color variations. 2-3/8" x 1-1/2". $175-350.

This antique gold tree is created from half loops set with gold balls. Larger gold balls embellish the setting around multi-colored stones (20). 2-1/4" x 1-1/2". $85-125.

This tree is old, with dark gold metal and candles (7) of single navettes where the metal is shaped like the candle. Marked. 2-5/8" x 1-1/2". $175-185.

Some refer to this as the "ribbon" tree. Here, long layered open branches extend downward from the top. The edges are beaded antique gold. Each branch is decorated with all green or all red stones (11). 2-1/4" x 1-3/4". $85-125.

The tiers have scrolled wire between a rope garland. Graduated clear rhinestones in an unusual cut makes this tree really sparkle. The base is stylized like a trunk and the top of the tree is plain metal sprayed white. 1-3/4" x 2-1/4". $85-150.

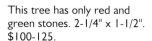

This tree has only red and green stones. 2-1/4" x 1-1/2". $100-125.

This tree has only rhinestones. Unmarked. 2-1/4" x 1-1/2". $35-50.

Two similar trees, except for stone colors, in antique brass. A raised rhinestone (20) and gold-ball garland winds itself across the tree four times. Large chatons decorate each section. The base is a deeply grooved triangle. 2-3/8" x 1-5/8". $125-150 each.

Similar to those preceding but in silver with clear stones. 2-3/8" x 1-5/8". $125-150.

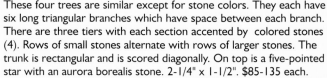

A trio of similar trees, except for stones and metals used. These trees have five long alternating V-sections, three forward and two recessed, which give dimension to the design. This one has multi-colored chatons (14). The pot looks like a real Christmas tree stand. 2-1/4" x 1-1/2". $100-125.

These four trees are similar except for stone colors. They each have six long triangular branches which have space between each branch. There are three tiers with each section accented by colored stones (4). Rows of small stones alternate with rows of larger stones. The trunk is rectangular and is scored diagonally. On top is a five-pointed star with an aurora borealis stone. 2-1/4" x 1-1/2". $85-135 each.

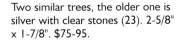

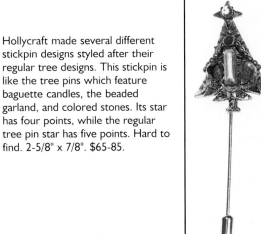

Hollycraft made several different stickpin designs styled after their regular tree designs. This stickpin is like the tree pins which feature baguette candles, the beaded garland, and colored stones. Its star has four points, while the regular tree pin star has five points. Hard to find. 2-5/8" x 7/8". $65-85.

Two similar trees, the older one is silver with clear stones (23). 2-5/8" x 1-7/8". $75-95.

A newer gold tree uses aurora borealis stones (23). It was bought in 1998. The mark is unclear. 2-5/8" x 1-7/8". $35-55.

Two trees of similar design with the layout of stones (24) the same. One tree has been enameled white and has a flatter tree trunk. 2-1/2" x 1-3/8". $60-125 each.

A trio of similar candle trees by Hollycraft. They have a raised beaded garland. There are tall baguette candles (5) made of one stone (except for the blue one which uses two smaller baguettes per candle), with a rhinestone flame. Two different size ornaments (12) line the bottom and are distributed throughout the tree. A simple trunk is turned slightly upward at the bottom. Although these trees are of similar style, they look different because of their colored stones. 2" x 1-1/2". $115-150 each.

A wonderful old tree with branches deeply textured and flat. Seven clear baguette candles with red enamel flames and multi-colored stones cover the branches. This design is also made by Pakula. Found marked and unmarked. 2-1/4" x 1-5/8". $150-275.

Here is a lovely tree which can be worn all year long. The colors used are truly characteristic of Hollycraft. Different size stones and scroll work make this piece truly stunning. Pronged. Mark indistinct: Hollycraft CORP. or HOLLYCRAFT. 1950. 2" x 1-1/2". $85-150.

A wonderful candle tree similar to one shown previously except for the candle's flame. 2-1/4" x 1-5/8". $85-150.

This is the "Bow Tie" tree. It uses cinnamon red bow ties with clear rhinestone centers. Pakula also made this style tree. 2-1/8" x 1-5/8". $65-75.

Here is a fanciful reindeer "tree". The deer itself is enamel with a rhinestone harness. The tail is goldtone, the eye is a "Rudolph" red stone. The deer's antlers become the tree's branches decorated with colored stones (6) and 2 dangling pears. 1-3/4" x 1-1/4". $80-95.

Here are six trees in four different styles, all using the same ornate pot.

Two trees of textured rope garlands, one with dark aurora borealis stones and the other with pastel stones. 2-1/2" x 1-1/2". $90-150 each.

The design is the "Flower Tree" with stacked flowers filled with different colored stones. 2-3/8" x 1-1/2". $45-65 each.

A petal tree in layers and tiers. Each tier is outlined in white and uses clear rhinestones (15). 2-1/2" x 1-1/2". $50-100.

Fran B. Hurst
1998 ~ 2002

Fran Basden Hurst

Fran and Michael Hurst exhibit and sell jewelry primarily at art and craft festivals in Florida and Michigan. They also sell in boutiques, shops, and on the internet.

Here are five fun pieces of jewelry. The metal is molded and decorated with sparkling stones, dangling glass beads, and interesting topical pieces. The shape and size stays the same on all pieces. Each tree has a title. Marked on their cards only.

This tree is created from many open cut branches. There are two layers where each branch is bent slightly forward. 2-5/8" x 1-1/2". $75-125.

The Butterfly Christmas Tree. 3" x 1-1/2". $25-45.

The 2000 New Year's Eve Tree. 2-1/2" x 1-15/16". $25-45.

Two pins where a colored stone sits in the middle of a rope circle with six gold leaves radiating outward. This creates a flower design. One has aurora borealis stones. Unmarked. 2-1/4" x 1-1/2". $45-75 each.

The Angel and Flower Tree. 2-7/8" x 1-1/2". $25-45.

The Flamingo Christmas Tree. 2-1/2" x 1-3/4". $25-45.

The Turtle Christmas tree. 2-1/16" x 1-1/4". All new 2000. $25-45.

JA

John Avery (JA) of Craftsman, Inc., Kerrville, Texas works in sterling silver.

The peace (PAX) tree has a lamb, a lion, and a bird. 1-5/8" x 1-1/8". $45-60.

JD / DJ
1998-2002

Joyce Yost is an artist who lives in Jackson, Michigan.

A snowy tree accented with differently sized blue balls. This is made using a 12-layer craft process where the design is hand painted and layered with clear resin. The back looks like gold paint. Sold in boutique shops. Marked on the card only. 1999. 2-5/8" x 2". $25-35.

Jeanne

Here is a cute little reindeer tree. He is goldtone with tiny green stone eyes. His antlers have small dangling glass balls in red and green (4). 1-7/8" x 1-1/2". $40-50.

Jezlaine

A circle pin holding a snowman and a Christmas tree. The tree has green enamel with a yellow star. The snowman has a red enamel scarf. The pin is made of sterling silver. It says, "Merry Xmas." Marked. Diameter: 1-1/4". Sold originally for $40. $40-60.

J.J.
1935 - 2002

The J. J. Company was founded in 1935 as the Providence Jewelry Company. After World War II, Abraham Lisker renamed his company after his mother and father and it become the Jonette Company.

J. J. has specialized, for a long time, in novelty pins. However, Christmas pins have become a speciality of theirs. JJ designed a wide range of holiday pins. There are trees with a Santa, a sleigh, an angel, and trees with cats or mice, a car with a tree, and many other designs. Many of the JJ trees are small, but later, as shown here, there was a larger and more ornate line created.

A stylized tree with branches on the left that swoop downward ending in a curl with a rhinestone on the curl's edge. The other side is a traditional design with rhinestones (6). 2-1/2" x 1-7/8". $45-55.

This tree is the simplest of this group of three in plain goldtone and colored stones. 1-7/8" x 1-3/8". $25-35.

A most unusual design. This is a little boy's Christmas tree with a drum, angel, candle, present, elephant, horse, candy cane, teddy bear, and toy horn. These images are slightly raised and are strung together by a garland which is highlighted with multi-colored cabochons (6). The body of the tree is textured gold. Another unusual feature is that of 50 plus JJ trees shown here, it is the only one to have a date on it. 1986. 2-1/2" x 1-5/8". $55-65.

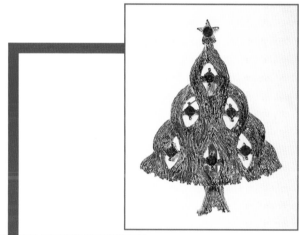

The following three trees have the same overall design but differ in metal color and enamel. All have stones (6) set in an open diamond design. The body is highly textured, giving it the appearance of being woven. 1-3/4" x 1-1/2". $25-35 each.

The following six trees all have the same little star with a single stone at the top. The following three trees are the same design, a simple half tier with an open area between each tier. They have different trunks. This tree is the fanciest one, with a cutout star design around each colored stone. 1-7/8" x 1-3/8". $25-35.

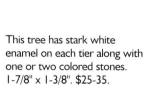

This tree has stark white enamel on each tier along with one or two colored stones. 1-7/8" x 1-3/8". $25-35.

These cat's have had their dream come true. Here they enjoy a tree covered with one of their favorite foods...fish. The tree top also features a fish. Notice the skeleton of an eaten fish in the middle of the tree. Multi-colored stones add color to this gold tone pin. Cat lovers will greatly enjoy the humor. 3-1/4" x 1-7/8". $10-20.

This is similar to the preceding pin but in a bright gold metal. 1-3/4" x 1-1/2". $35-50.

A cute little mouse carrying a tree slung over his back. Accents are in red and white enamel with one tiny green stone for the mouse's eye. 1-3/8" x 1-1/2". $30-35.

A larger tree using three horizontal tiers. The edge of the tiers is created by using navettes (17), in slightly raised setting. 2-3/8" x 1-5/8". $50-65.

This snow covered tree in white enamel looks pretty. The snow has a glitter and the branches stick out from under the snow. 1-3/4" x 1-5/8". $10-20.

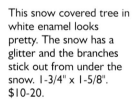

An antique brass tree in a deeply scrolled design. The six stones decorate the edge and a large oval stone sits in the middle. 1-3/4" x 1-1/2". $35-50.

Two similar scroll trees, one in bright gold tone and the other in antique brass. This scroll design has multi-colored stones (9). 1-3/4" x 1-1/2". $50-65 each.

This is a three tier tree using a lattice made from connecting diamond shapes. There are rows of tiny stones (30) which alternate with rows of stars. 2-3/8" x 1-3/4". $35-45.

These pins are a variation on one theme: a branch is a simple drooping petal with a rounded edge. Some have smooth edges, another a scalloped edge, and others have jagged edges.

This pin uses a single gold ball and colored stones (14) in each section with three additional tiny balls. 2-1/8" x 1-3/4". $35-45.

Here are seven tiers of individual petal branches. Each petal curves up and out holding a single gold ball or stone (15). The open work of the petals gives a nice delicate feeling to this design. 2-3/8" x 1-3/4". $35-45.

These two trees are similar except for differently colored stones. There are seven tiers in a simple scroll design across each tier. A gold ball alternates with a multi-colored stones (11). The edge of each tier is a slightly raised beaded design. 2-3/8" x 1-3/4". $35-45.

These four pins use six petal tiers. One has smooth edges while the others have jagged edges. A single stone decorates each tier. The surface variations include brushed gold, a green wash, a highly polished metal , and high polished with green enamel edges. 1-3/4" x 1-3/8". $25-35 each.

This tree is larger and more ornate than the others shown here. These half-tiers look like a fancy garland. Their edges are scalloped in a textured gold tone. The inside of each tier is cut away, and a small group of multi-colored stones (26) cluster like a bouquet of posies. 2-1/4" x 2". $45-60.

A tree with five diagonal tiers and a rhinestone (28) garland. 2-3/8" x 1-5/8". $35-55.

This tree has a downward diagonal design from left to right and four scalloped garlands with open stars. Colored rhinestones (17) sit between each garland, making a garland of their own. 2-1/4" x 1-5/8". $35-50.

Here Santa carries a Christmas tree, a basket of full of toys, and a horn on his belt. This pin is cast metal with enamel decoration. 2000. 2-1/8" x 1-1/8". $25-35.

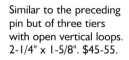

Similar to the preceding pin but of three tiers with open vertical loops. 2-1/4" x 1-5/8". $45-55.

This design has branches fanned out from the top with rhinestones evenly spaced. 2-1/4" x 1-7/8". $35-55.

This tree has downward diagonal tiers from right to left. Each tier has a slightly raised and polished edge and multi-colored stones (27). 2-1/4" x 2" . $35-55.

Similar tree to the preceding but with differently colored stones. 2-1/4" x 1-7/8". $35-55.

The following five trees use horizontal tiers. The first two resemble a Medieval troubadour's hat with the points in each tier having a tiny colored stone (12) on its tip. One is in a green wash while the other is in goldtone. 1-1/2" x 1-5/8". $50-65 each.

These three trees have green enamel on each tier with a garland of rhinestones set in gold or silver. This design is similar to one by Weiss. 2-1/2" x 1-3/4". $45-60 each.

What a delightful, whimsical Santa tree. It has rolly-polly eyes, a red and white enamel hat, and a jingle bell that dangles from the top of the hat. There are tiny stones (7) decorating the bottom tier, and two more for Santa's cheeks. 1-7/8" x 1-3/8". $75-90.

These two trees are taller than the others and have six tiers. One is antique gold and the other has a green wash. The metal is grooved and has colored stones (16) sprinkled on each tier. 2-1/4"-1-5/8". $40-55 each.

This design is a similar design to the preceding pins but with gold enamel on each tier. 2-1/2" x 1-3/4". $45-60.

Two similar trees except for the colors of the metal and the stones. Needled branches shoot downward holding many different colored stones (20). 2-1/4" x 1-5/8". $35-45 each.

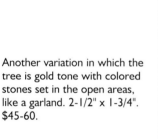

This design was often used by JJ with cut out half-tiers which overlap. Different colors and stone shapes are used. 2-1/8" x 2". $35-45.

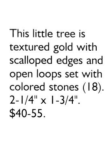

A tree with five tiers which are cut out and bent up and out. Multi-colored stones (21) and gold balls are sprinkled over the tiers. 2-1/2" x 1-7/8". $35-45.

Another variation in which the tree is gold tone with colored stones set in the open areas, like a garland. 2-1/2" x 1-3/4". $45-60.

This little tree is textured gold with scalloped edges and open loops set with colored stones (18). 2-1/4" x 1-3/4". $40-55.

This tree uses three rows of tiny gold balls around the tree's edge. Tiny stones (35) decorate each tier. 2-1/8" x 1-1/2". $35-45 each.

On a wire-style frame, this tree is covered with multi-colored stones (37), including purple. 2-1/4" x 1-3/4". $30-40.

Two similar trees whose edges are beaded and swoop upward in loops. Each loop holds a colored stone (6). One tree has a green wash while the other is in an antique textured gold finish. c. 1950s-1960s. 1-3/4" x 1-1/2". $35-45 each.

Each tier has a scalloped edge. It uses an open scroll design with a tiny colored stone (8) in the curl of the design. c. 1950s-1960s. 1-3/4" x 1-1/2". $35-45.

This tree has a green wash and a jagged edge. One tiny rhinestone (6) sits in each section of the tiers. c. 1950s-1960s. 1-3/4" x 1-1/2". $35-45.

Two similar trees, one in brushed gold and the other with a green wash. Each tier has a scalloped edge. The tiers are created from stylized rectangles, with one stone in each section (12). c. 1950s-1960s. 1-3/4" x 1-1/2". $35-45 each.

A frog grinch stole this Christmas tree. 2000.
1-5/8" x 1-5/8". $15-20.

Coming home for Christmas. 2000. 3" x 1-5/8". $15-20.

The old "woody" with our tree on top. 2000. 2-1/4" x
1-3/8". $15-20.

Tree and toys dangle from Santa. 2000. 2-3/4" x 2-1/2". $20-25.

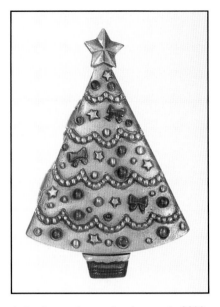

A simple tree in metal and enamel. 2000.
2-7/8" x 2-1/4". $15-25.

The hinged pin opens to reveal a scene with Santa inside the house.

Topiary tree. 2000.
2-1/2" x 7/8". $15-25.

Two similar trees using a left-to-right diagonal design. There are four tiers with open circles holding tiny stones (7) which look like balls. 1-3/4" x 1-3/8". $25-35.

A tree with three horizontal tiers. An open loop in each tier holds a tiny stone. Eight clear rhinestones hang below each separated tier. 1-7/8" x 1-5/8". $25-35.

A jaunty Santa cat holding a tree over his shoulder like an umbrella. 1-1/2" x 1-1/4". $75-100.

A cute little angel holding up a tree as though walking in a procession. 1-3/4" x 1-1/2". $45-60.

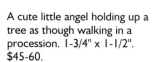

JK

A charming tree which reminds one of the Kirk's Folly pin designs. All kinds of interesting articles create this tree: a butterfly, a moon, a heart, two stars, a skate, a clock, and a crown. The stars, heart, moon, and butterfly have rhinestones recessed in them. Several pearls are scattered over the surface. Two marks on the back: JK and Made in USA. 2-3/8" x 1-5/8". $35-45.

js

A tree with green enamel, gold bows, and red and gold stones. 3" x 2-1/2". $ 15-25.

Judith Jack

JUDITH JACK for Jacobson's

A wonderfully detailed tree in sterling. It has three rows of silver hearts above a band of silver. Red and green stones (10) add color. Same style star sits on top. New 1999. 1-1/2" x 3/4". $65-100.

Jurgensen
1999 ~ 2002

Judith Jurgensen was born in 1950 in Louisville, Kentucky and started her business making jewelry in 1999. She wanted to make extra money so she could travel with her daughter who is a photographer. She sells on e-bay.

Carved cameo set in silver frame. Signed in script: J J 2000. 2" x 1-3/4". $25-35.

Justwin
1900s~2002

Justwin is a German company currently in production and selling primarily in European countries.

The tree is a clear intaglio plaque in reverse and hand painted. It has a stamped gold tone frame. The plaque is set with Swarovski stones. Pronged. Late 1990s. 1-1/2" x 3/4". $65-90.

K & T

A group of three molded trees in relief. One tree is silver, one is copper, and one is bronze color. The packages at the bottom of the silver and bronze trees are in red, blue, and green enamel. 2-1/8" x 2-1/4". $10-15.

Kirks Folly
1979 ~ 2002

"Dream and Believe" is the philosophy the Kirks Folly family credit with helping them achieve their goals. This family of magic-makers delights in bringing fanciful images of angels, fairies, sun, moon, stars, wizards and sea creatures to life as wearable art. It's been a magical ride for the whimsical collection that was created merely, as Helen says, "to help people smile again."

The angels were smiling in 1979 when Helen Kirk made some rhinestone-glittered chignon chopsticks. Her sister Jenniefer thought they were terrific and boldly took them to Bloomingdale's. The sisters got right behind the counter and drew a captivated audience with their demonstration of how to wear them. The result was pure Kirk magic with the store's buyer declared, "I'll buy anything you make."

The business was literally born at the kitchen table with family members hand assembling their creations. "However, orders piled-up and we knew that we had to get serious," says Jenniefer. They recruited sister Elizabeth and brother George, and the four siblings combined their talents to form a winning team.

None of the four had any business or art training. Elizabeth is a registered nurse, Helen has a masters degree in speech therapy, George had just graduated from college, and Jenniefer, of course, has a doctorate degree in "fairy dust!" Lack of experience didn't stop the dedicated foursome. "We built this business from pure determination and hard work. If you can dream it and believe it, you can do it!" declares Jenniefer.

Kirks Folly likes to title its Christmas trees. Unless the buyer or seller knows this, the title gets lost, like many marker's marks. Limited Edition pins are usually larger than the rest of the line and have a safety guard on the back. *(Used with permission of Kirks Folly.)*

"Santa's On His Way." Here we see the six large red pear-shaped stones representing continents, stars, or constellations. The round green chatons might be the land around it. The chain shows the pathways that Santa must take to deliver his gifts. Limited Edition. Pronged. 1998. 4 -1/4" x 3". $185-250.

"A Partridge In A Pear Tree." A wonderful, large, glitzy partridge pin. The partridge is clear rhinestones except for a tear-drop beak. The tree's leaves are tiny green round stones with a navette set in the middle of each, and six shiny gold pears hanging down. The tree's trunk is made of two shades of amber chatons. Limited Edition. Pronged. 3-5/8" x 3-3/8". $225-300.

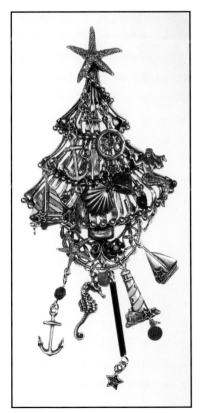

A silver tone tree which might be called "Sailing over the Bounding Main." Here three tiers of open branches are decorated with a dangling wheel, shell, anchor, bell, mermaid, sailboat, fish, starfish, lighthouse, etc. A bit of enamel and two cobalt blue stones are the only color. A large starfish of aurora borealis sits on top. 4-1/2" x 2-1/4". $55-70.

"Romance Tree." Here is real romance in a Christmas tree pin. Ruby hearts encased in gold lace and a double row of emerald green stones. A rhinestone stem rests in the red and clear rhinestone pot. Limited Edition 62/500. Pronged. 3-7/8" x 2-5/8". $225-300.

"Millenium Tree." Stunning! That's the only word to describe this pin. It is created with the Millennium colors of silver and blue. Tear-drop loops in rhinestones with aurora borealis dangles. Limited Edition. 1999. 5 -1/4" x 2-3/8". $250-275.

"O Christmas Tree." A tree with eight tiers of green stones, each tier layered above the last. The top bends slightly backwards for balance. The tip of the branches are set with a single red stone. Limited Edition. 1998. Pronged. 3-1/2" x 2-3/8". $125-150.

"Silent Night." Dangles and shimmers! There are five tiers of green stones. The branches are made of four stones dangling from three other stones. The three bottom tiers all shimmer and shake like the stars from the heavens above on that glorious night long years ago. Like the tree above, a single red stone sits on the tip of many branches. A large star, filled with six aurora borealis stones, sits on top. Limited Edition. 1998. Pronged. 3 -1/2" x 1-1/2". $125-150.

"Christmas Wizard." Here is the Christmas wizard in all his glory with flowing robes outlined in rhinestones and a rhinestone hat. Dangling from his chains are a snowflake, an enameled tree, a smaller snowflake with a red stone dangle, and two green orbs. His right hand is placing a wreath on top of the Christmas tree. The tree itself has green enameled branches with red stones (7), and an aurora borealis dangle. Pronged. 1998. 2-1/2" x 2-3/4". $60-75.

"Toyland Christmas Tree." The Toyland tree is designed similarly to the "O Christmas Tree" Limited Edition. This tree features six dangling stars on its looped branches. Dangling from the bottom is a rocking horse, a doll, a catcher's mitt, a toy soldier, and a bicycle. (It could be called "The Toy Tree.") It also comes in a larger size. Mark is in block letters. Pronged. 2-7/8" x 1-1/2". $55-75.

Kirk's Folly Holiday Pin Series:
1993: Baby's 1st Christmas Tree
1994: Teddy Bear Sleigh Ride Pin
1995: Frosty the Snowman Pin
1996: Angel Bell Pin
1997: Angels on High Pin
1998: Snowflake Pin

"The Gambler's Tree." This is a tree for those with a sense of humor and the desire to be different. Kirk's Folly offers a pin for the gambler. Three tiers of open rectangular branches have dangles of three aurora borealis stones, two dice, and three money bags. The top is a woman's hand holding four cards (heart, diamond, club, spade). 2-3/4" x 2". $55-75.

"Baby's 1st Christmas Tree." This style was used also on the Steadfast Soldier Tree. It is part of the Kirk's Folly Holiday Pin Series. Hanging from the bottom is a baby's cup, a dolly, stars, a heart, and a baby's block. 1993. 1-3/4" x 3". $50-65.

"School House Rock Pin." Kirk's Folly never lacks for new ideas for their jewelry. Here is a silver tree set with aurora borealis stones. A fairy sets a red enameled apple at the top of the tree under the star. A little school house with a red roof, a child's head, a globe, a bell, a computer, ruler, candy cane in red and white, scissors, and a diploma with several additional jeweled stars complete this magical pin. What fun! 1999. 1-3/4" x 3-1/4". $55-75.

"The South Beach Tree Pin." For beach lovers everywhere! Enameled dolphins (6), with stars and sea shells. Aurora borealis stones and opaque "pearls" (6) dangle from the shells. 3-1/2" x 1-1/2". $65-90.

"Nutcracker Ballet." From Tchaikovsky to Kirk's Folly, for Ballet lovers everywhere. There are twirling ballerinas, the sugar plum fairy, a toy soldier, and the mouse king's crown. Set with aurora borealis stones. 3-1/4" x 2". $55-75.

"The Creepy Crawler Tree." A slightly arched tree of interlocking diamonds with aurora borealis stones (20) recessed in each. Crawling all over the tree is wildlife: a spider with rhinestones, a lavender and blue lady bug, a bird in blue and yellow enamel, three enameled butterflies in different sizes, and an enameled dragonfly at the bottom. The star on top is of lavender enamel with a clear rhinestone in the middle. Absolutely wonderful and creative. Could be worn anytime. 2-3/4" x 1-1/2". $55-75.

"Sparkle's First Christmas." Look carefully and you'll find three enameled cats, a cat's head, a mouse, butterflies, a bee, and a beetle. At the bottom is a three-dimensional cat with wings, a cat's paw, and a sock. 3-1/4" x 1-1/2". $65-90.

"The Victorian Tree." A silver tree made of flowers with seven aurora borealis centers. Bows set with silver balls and rhinestones sit atop the flowers. Five aurora borealis stones sparkle in the tree's pot. 1998. 2-1/4" x 1-5/8". $45-60.

"Toy Christmas Tree." Toys dangle beneath a simple tree, which is the same style as "Baby's First Christmas." 3-1/2" x 1-1/2". $35-50.

"Star Tree." A flat tree of 15 overlapping gold stars of the same size and a tiny one on top of the tree. 1998. 1-7/8" x 1-15/16". $25-40.

"Victoriana Tree." Here is an old fashioned Christmas tree made of roses with aurora borealis centers, pink hearts, and a dove with a sprig of greenery. There are swags of beads and crystals. An embossed puffed heart charm with lovebirds and a green crystal dangle beneath this tree. 1-7/8" x 4". $45-60.

"We Three Kings." Here a series of stacked hearts are set with emerald green stones and a medium-sized clear rhinestone is attached to the top of each heart. A star-cut rhinestone sits on top. Limited Edition. 2-7/8" x 2-1/2". $100-125.

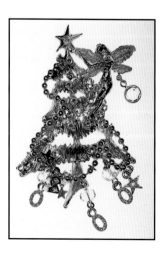

"Millennium Magic." Dangling from the bottom of this tree are the numbers 2-0-0-0. The tree sparkles with the magic of the New Year and the new millennium. It is set with aurora borealis stones, a garland of rhinestones, and a loose garland of gold balls. An angel places a star on top of the tree and stars and crystals hang from the bottom. 1999. 3-1/4" x 1-3/4". $60-75.

"Starry Nights." Individual branches hang downward with rhinestones (15) between each one. There are individual stars (7) in different sizes (including the one on the top of the tree) which are set with numerous stones (34). The star next to the top is a "shooting star." This tree twinkles like a night full of stars. 1998. 2-3/8" x 1-3/4". $45-55.

Anne Klein II

"The Angel Tree." An extremely interesting 1998 design. The top two angels are in flight and are viewed from the side; the bottom left tree has angels playing a harp while the right one holds a bow and arrow. The center angel faces forward . Five aurora borealis stones are in the pin itself, six are in the star, and four dangle from the bottom. 2-1/2" x 2-1/8". $50-65.

This tree has 25 stacked stars in eight tiers. Each star is adorned with a clear stone in it's middle. A single stone is on top and a gold bow is on the bottom. Unmarked except for box which is marked ANNE KLEIN II. 1999. 2-1/2" x 1-3/8". $25-35.

This is an older angel tree whose name has become lost. The finish is antique gold, not shiny like the one above. It has 14 tiny angels (all similar in design) which are stacked in tiers with arms outstretched. One hand of each angel holds a single rhinestone (15). The top of the tree is an angel also, but is not well formed. 2-1/4" x 1-5/8". $45-55.

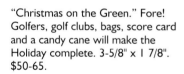

"Christmas on the Green." Fore! Golfers, golf clubs, bags, score card and a candy cane will make the Holiday complete. 3-5/8" x 1 7/8". $50-65.

A tree whose tiers are made of loops set with a colored stone (24) in the bottom of each loop. A simple gold star on top. Unmarked except for box which is marked ANNE KLEIN II. 1999. 2-1/2" x 1-1/2". $25-35.

Branches shaped like tear drops of green stones enclosing one ruby red stone create this tree. Its open work and swinging stars are dynamic. Gold stars (20) with clear rhinestones (6) dangle from the tree. Limited Edition 265/300. Pronged. 1998. 5-1/4" x 2-1/2". $185-225.

A cute little tree with seven tiers of layered green enameled branches. A goldtone banner with 1999 is strung across the middle of the tree. Mark: AK. 1999. 2" x 1-1/2". $45-60.

Bonnie Kondor
1999 ~ 2002

A great pin of new three dimensional art made by using a print of a famous painting coated with polymer. Grant Wood's *American Gothic* farmer holds a Christmas tree instead of a pitchfork in this pin. Also, the farmer wears Santa's hat with a pearl tassle. The tree is decorated with glass beads and acrylic jewels. Designed and created by Bonnie Kondor of Lake Forest, Illinois. 2000. 2-5/8" x 1-3/8". $35-45.

A green tree with white snow. Trimmed with multi-colored stones and pearls. 1-7/8" x 1-1/4". $65-75.

Aurora borealis stones with jewel tone dangles (8). 2-1/8" x 1-3/4". $150-200.

Kramer
1943 ~ late 1970s

Kramer Jewelry Creations was founded by Louis Kramer in 1943. Kramer also produced jewelry for Christian Dior which were marked "Dior by Kramer." Marks: Kramer, Kramer of New York.

A rhinestone tree with seven green baguette candles and red flames. Green stones (12) create the pot. 2-1/2" x 2". $150-180.

This tree has gold enameled edges with a pattern of multi-colored stones. Comes in other colors. 2-1/4" x 1-5/8". $175-200.

Krementz
1884 ~ 2002

A mushroom cap tree of four tiers with colored stones. Mark can be seen only under magnification. 1-1/2" x 1-1/8". $25-35.

A highly stylized tree with eight randomly scattered jewels. Thought to be one of a few trees made by Krementz. 1-1/2"-1-1/4". $85-100.

Rhinestones set in three tiers of "L's" are topped off with small red stones. Marked: Kenneth Lane. 2-3/4" x 1-5/8". $70-85.

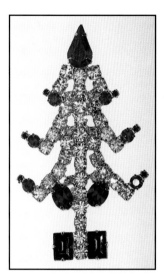

Kenneth J. Lane
1963 - 2002

Kenneth J. Lane (K.J.L.) has been a trend setter in jewelry. His list of awards for design go on and on. He has designed for the Metropolitan Museum of Art, Avon, and the Trump Tower. He also sells abroad.

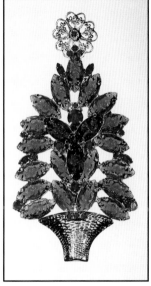

Bright green stones (22) with silver basket. 2000. 4" x 2". $35-50.

A wonderful tree created out of five tiers of navettes (28) in gem tones. A ruby red pear shape sits as the tree's star. The typical "packages" are at the base of the tree. Marked: KENNETH LANE. 2-7/8" x 1-7/8". $60-75.

This tree design has been used also by both Eisenberg and Swarovsky. Who used it first? Rows of emerald green and clear chatons glimmer while surrounded by larger green, blue, and purple ones. There are also emerald cut stones (4 red, 1 clear), and a single pear on top. Pronged. Gold backing. 2-5/8" x 2-1/8". $75-85.

Here the stones are chatons (12) and navettes in tiers which alternate between the different shapes. Marked: KJL. 2-7/8" x 2". $70-85.

Four tiers of clear chatons are enclosed in a multi-pronged setting. The trunk uses 2 long navette "packages" and a large green emerald cut stone. Pronged. Silver. Marked: Kenneth Lane. 2-1/2" x 1-3/4". $75-85.

Similar to a previous tree, this one has narrow branches swooping downward in clear rhinestones (22). Red stones (13) create the tree's spine topped by a red pear-shaped stone. Multi-colored chatons and navettes decorate the limbs. Pronged. Silver. 2-3/4" x 1-3/4". $75-85.

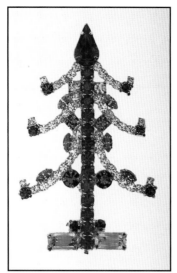

A combination of pink frosted stones and clear green stones. The top four rows use pear stones and the bottom two rows have navettes. 2000. 3-1/2" x 2". $65-80.

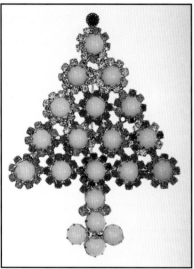

Here are what I call KJL's "Snow Tree." Round milky stones (20) create the center of jewel tone flowers (15) in five tiers. A small green chaton resides on top and balances the one green flower directly below it at the bottom of the tree. Gold backed. Pronged. 3-1/8" x 2-1/4". $70-85.

A different look with a taste of lemon pie. Here are four rows plus a star of small lemon yellow stones. Garlands of aurora borealis hang between them. This tree has zap due to the strength of the stones' color. 2000. 2-1/2" x 1-1/2". $50-65.

Milky navettes (10) create the center of these flowers in an oval loop. Red and green stones (8 per flower) are used in four tiers. Note the artistic use of turquoise stones on the bottom of the trunk. Top stone is not encased, but pronged. Silver backed. 2-3/8" x 1-5/8". $60-75.

This has the same design as a previous tree, but in dark ruby, light blue, and medium blue stones. Looks patriotic with its white trunk. 2000. 3-1/2" x 2". $65-80.

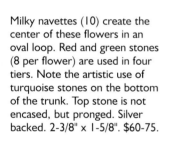

Just to look at this tree one would would say it was KJL. However, it is unmarked. Milky navettes are horizontally stacked creating five tiers. They alternate with tiny jewel tone stones. Emerald cut stones form presents under the tree. Pronged. 2-1/4" x 2". $50-65.

A combination of green glass navettes with dangling milky-white glass stones in six tiers create this tree. Silver star on top. 2000. 3-1/2" x 2". $65-80.

A tree of pale pink navettes (15) surrounded by rhinestones (13) in three layers. 2000. 3-1/2" x 2-1/8". $75-90.

LIA

Lia stands for Lianna, Inc. of Cranston, Rhode Island. They also produce the "Fancy That" line of jewelry.

Here are dark stones with red candles (6), amber flames, and aurora borealis balls. Pronged. 2000. 3-1/8" x 2-3/4". $70-85.

A squat, multi-colored tree created by different types and sizes of stones. 2000. 2-3/4" x 2-1/8". $35-50.

A wonderful design that originated in the 1930s in gold and diamonds. This is the costume version. Here graduated branches rise from a base and the front of each branch is set with rhinestones. A single stone is set on each edge. 3" x 2". $150-185 each.

A tree of green cabochons (18) with a garland of dangling metal chain. 2000. 3-1/8" x 1-7/8". $45-55.

A small tree in silver and gold tones with a gold star sits on top. Tiny red and green stones (6) are on the edge of each tier. 2-1/8" x 1-1/8". $15-25.

An interesting tree using stars with stones (6) and gold balls in circles. 2-1/8" x 1-1/2". $15-25.

Tree with colored stones of clear to dark Montana blue. 3" x 1-3/4". $60-75.

A thin garland crisscrosses the green enamel to make seven tiers. Clear stones (8) dot each section of the tree. 2-1/2" x 1-1/2". $25-35.

This tree is made of six wonderful poinsettia flowers. The flowers have enameled red petals with green leaves. A single rhinestone is in the center of each flower. 2" x 1-1/8". $35-45.

A bow tree that uses ten green enameled bows in an open rectangular shape. Resting between the bows are red enameled balls (5) and a single gold ball. 2-1/8" x 2". $25-35.

A small tree with four tiers of circular flowers. Each has a center of an enameled ball. 2-1/2" x 1-1/2". $15-25.

The following four trees all have a solid metal star on top and similar trunk design.

A wonderful tree with red, green, and clear stones in graduated sizes. It is packed together with nine tiny gold stars. 4" x 1-1/2". $50-65.

A tailored tree with six rows of baguettes (21) in traditional holiday colors. Stones are edged in gold tone metal. These baguettes are stacked with space between them. 3" x 1-3/8". $45-55.

A silver tree is created from rope ovals, each set with a single stone or silver ball. 2-1/2" x 1-1/2". $20-30.

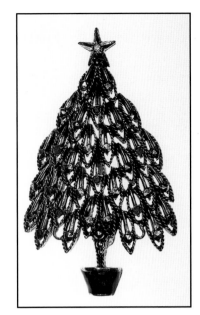

A small tree filled with various sized stones in red, green, and clear 13). 2-1/4" x 1-1/2". $25-35.

Here five tiers of navettes are joined with gold balls. Traditional colors are used. 3" x 1-3/8". $30-45.

A green enamel tree outlined with gold balls. Red enamel balls sit on three of the four tiers. 2-1/4" x 1-3/4". $15-20.

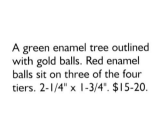

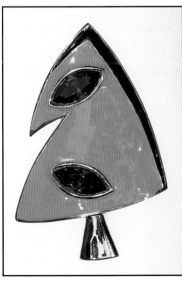

Kathy Flood designed this tree for the Linnart Collection. It is called "Pinecasso," after the great artist Pablo Picasso. It is a Limited Edition. Kathy calls this enamel color "seafoam green." The two large Montana blue marquis stones are set in silverplate. The pin is signed LIA. 1999. 2-1/2" x 1-3/4". $100-110.

Small tree made with red and green enameled packages. Rhinestones highlight the pin. 1-7/8" x 1-5/8". $20-30.

Three trees of similar design with different stone colors and metals. There are five half tiers that cross and are set with colored stones (13). 2" x 1-5/8". $20-30 each.

A teardrop tree of red, green, and clear stones (10). 2-7/16" x 1-1/2". $35-45.

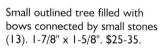

Small outlined tree filled with bows connected by small stones (13). 1-7/8" x 1-5/8". $25-35.

A marcasite-looking tree with red and green stones (5). 2-1/8" x 1-3/8". $20-30.

A red garland crosses this tree. Green and gold balls hang between the garland and four packages hang from the bottom. 2-5/8" x 1-3/8". $25-35.

A tree of layered pine needle branches with colored stones (12). 2-5/8" x 2-1/8". $25-35.

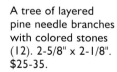

A swirling red enameled ribbon creates a tree in four tiers. Red, green and clear stones (5) hang from different parts of the ribbon. A solid metal star is on top. 2-1/2" x 1-1/2". $25-35.

A tailored tree in green enamel with a red band crossing down its center. Rhinestones (4) add a bit of glitter. 2-1/4" x 1-1/2". $25-35.

This three tier tree has textured green enamel and is outlined in a gold rope garland with tiny balls hanging down. A single rhinestone is in the top star with a metal circle behind it. 2-5/8" x 1-5/8". $25-35.

A realistic tree of prickly needles set with differently colored stones (14). 1999. 2-1/8" x 1-3/4". $20-35.

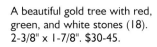

A beautiful gold tree with red, green, and white stones (18). 2-3/8" x 1-7/8". $30-45.

A pretty poinsettia tree recreated by LIA using a plastic for the flowers and enamel for the leaves. (An earlier version was created in metal and enamel.) 2-1/2" x 2". $35-45.

A charming feline all decked out in a green enamel dress with rope accessories and red enamel buttons. Her hat, along with the dress, create the tree. 2-7/8" x 1-5/8". $25-35.

A silver tree made with bells hanging from the branches. The bells' clappers are tiny stones (9). 2" x 1-1/2". $25-35.

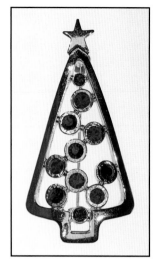

A simple triangular tree with a group of red and green stones that create the interior design. 2-1/4" x 1-1/8". $15-20.

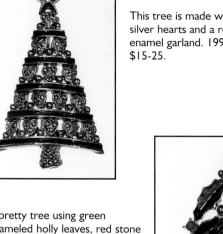

This tree is made with five rows of silver hearts and a red and green enamel garland. 1999. 2-1/8" x 1-1/2". $15-25.

A silver tree whose four tiers run diagonally. A tiny garland of red, blue, and green stones parallel the tiers. 2-1/8" x 1-1/2". $20-30.

A pretty tree using green enameled holly leaves, red stone berries (7), and gold balls. 1999. 2" x 1-3/4". $15-25.

A green enamel tree with rhinestone (7) balls and a star on top. 1999. 2-5/8" x 1-5/8". $15-20.

Four tiers of branches in an open design filled with multi-colored stones (8). 1999. 2" x 1-3/4". $15-25.

Stacked open diamond shapes create this tree of goldtone metal with clear rhinestones (14). 2-1/4" x 1-3/4". $15-25.

A gold tree with green enamel leaves. The tree has six red and six clear stones. 1999. 2" x 1-1/2". $25-40.

This tree of open diamond shapes which uses silver with red and green stones (14). A single stone sits in the base of the tree's trunk and one in the star. 2-1/4" x 1-3/4". $15-25.

Don Lin

Don Lin's pins can be found in the Texas department stores.

A cute enameled tree in two sections with red and gold balls, two packages, and a bear that dangles. 3-1/2" x 2-3/8". $25-35

The Southwestern theme is shown here in a cactus Christmas tree. 1-1/4" x 1". $15-25.

These trees are similar in style with five layers of projecting textured branches. One is enameled with pastel stones while the other uses traditionally colored stones (22). 2" x 1-1/2". $50-65 each.

A small tree with pronged branches shooting upward. Nice open work helps give elegance to this tree. Decorated with red navettes (5), green (11) and clear (11) stones. Red navette in the base. 2-1/2" x 1-7/8". $75-110.

Lisner

1938 ~ 1985

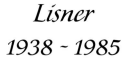

The Lisner company was founded in 1938. However, it did not mark it's pieces until 1959. In the 1970s it became part of the Lisner-Richelieu Corporation.

A tree with five layers of projecting branches decorated with green, white and red stones (20). The base has two rhinestones. Comes unmarked also. 2-1/8" x 1-3/4". $50-65.

A Lisner design from the classic Warner and Eisenberg style tree. Stones are red, green, and clear. Candles (6) are clear baguettes with round red flames. 2-1/2" x 1-5/8". $50-75.

Springy loops in four tiers set with a red navette stones make this pin really unusual. The design gives a wonderful feeling of a tree with colored lights after a heavy snow. 2" x 1-3/4". $85-100.

Liz Ann

A beautiful molded silver tree with light blue stones (16). The tree is fairly heavy. 2-1/8" x 1-5/8". $25-35.

A layered tree with branches projecting to each side. Seven colored stones go down the middle in an alternating color pattern, with other stones on the branches. 2-1/2" x 1-1/2". $30-45.

Tiers of wire loops with colored stones (24). Trunk is a continuation of the wire loops. 2-1/2" x 1-5/8". $30-45.

A small textured tree in four tiers which are layered and bent forward for dimension. There are seven stones sprinkled over the tiers. Similar to a Coro design. 1-7/8" x 1-1/4". $30-40.

LJM

This is a fancy tree for LJM. Alternating branches with colored balls dot the center spine with a green stone on top. 2-1/4" x 1-1/4". $30-45.

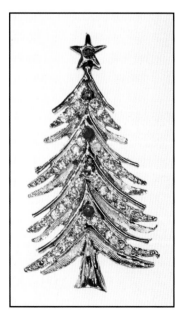

Similar to the top tree in design except no layering. 2" x 1-1/2". $25-35.

Very similar in style to Brook's "Harp" pin, but of lesser quality. Ten red and green balls hang from the limbs with a blue stone just above the trunk and a clear stone on the star. 2-1/4" x 1-7/8". $25-35.

Longaberger Baskets
1997 ~ 2002

LONGABERGER®

Longaberger basket company of Ohio has produced several Christmas tree pins. These are unsigned, but came on the Longaberger card. Don Paquette is their designer. New tree pins are available on a Longaberger card, but they are signed JJ.

These speciality tree pins are each decorated with four small Longaberger company hanging baskets. Note the basket for the pot. All metal. 1-1/2" x 2-1/2". $50-65 each.

Loret

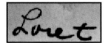

A charming ceramic tree with wrapped presents and a teddy bear. 2" x 2". $25-35.

Lunch at the Ritz
1982~2002

Esme Hecht wanted to be a writer, even though he studied art and sculpture in college. Alexis Watts trained to be a pianist. However, as fate would have it, in the 1970s they happen to meet in San Francisco and began working as street artists in order to pay their bills. They created jewelry in the closet of their apartment and sold it out of a cart on the street. These first pieces were in gold and silver using amethyst, turquoise and gemstones in Art Deco and Art Nouveau designs. Since their jewelry was not met with the enthusiasm they had hoped for, they considered returning to writing and music. However, they both missed creating jewelry and decided to change their designs into fun, whimsical pieces. They felt women wanted some fun in their lives and to show their individuality. How better to show one's personality than through one's jewelry?

In 1981, they moved to New York. Bad weather and the police became their worst adversaries. In 1982, they left New York City and moved to Germantown, New York. There they began again. In 1983, with a tiny booth at a boutique show, they introduced "Lunch at the Ritz." Their jewelry was now in brass and resin, because it was less expensive. Their designs were recognized as "high fashion."

In 1997, they decided to relocate to the town of Ulster, New York. They purchased four acres of land near the former IBM site which had been abandoned in 1993. There they have built, by hand, a new 15,000 square foot building to house their fifty employees. This facility is three times the size of their old building.

Each piece of jewelry starts out in brass with a base coat of 24 kt. gold or platinum silver. Then it is colored with a resin coating and hand painted with vibrant colors. Each piece is hand-drilled and cut out, which connects into another piece creating three-dimensional objects.

"Lunch" designs a new collection three times a year. Since the pieces have become highly collectible, there is not a long lifespan for any one piece, which may simply return with a change of color or stone setting for a whole new look. Everything in the line is about food: the catalog is the "Menu" with categories such as "Couture Entrees," "The Desserts," and "Fresh from the Garden." Each piece is also titled. Although they are known for their some 700 different earrings, they also make bracelets, belts, and necklaces. Prior to 1989, the pieces were signed by "Lunch at the Ritz." Today a plaque appears on the back of each piece.

They named the company Lunch at the Ritz because it sounds like fun and fancy all rolled into one. That is exactly what Esme and Alexis try to do, provide all their hungry customers with a taste of fun, elegance, and whimsy. (*Used with permission from "Lunch at the Ritz Earwear, Inc."*)

Three green resin frogs, each with a little red enamel and rhinestone Santa hat! Enamel and glass balls dangle from a 4-1/2" star in green and clear stones. Pronged. 5-1/2" x 2-1/4". $350-450.

Mamselle

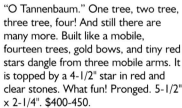

A tailored tree which has two layers of branches. A polished edge creates a lovely tree. Much like a Trifari design. A single pearl adorns the top. 2" x 1-3/8". $30-45.

"O Tannenbaum." One tree, two tree, three tree, four! And still there are many more. Built like a mobile, fourteen trees, gold bows, and tiny red stars dangle from three mobile arms. It is topped by a 4-1/2" star in red and clear stones. What fun! Pronged. 5-1/2" x 2-1/4". $400-450.

What a fun piece of jewelry this is. The tree itself is green with a large red star on top. Both are covered with resin. On the tree tiny enamel balls create a garland swag. A garland of rhinestones crisscrosses and dangles from the rhinestone star on top. Dangling balls, stars, beads, jewels, and a candy cane complete the picture. 3" x 2-3/16". $200-250.

Similar to the preceding tree except it has seven baguette candles, chatons (5), with a rhinestone on top. 2" x 1-3/8". $45-60.

A little tree of half tiers in red, yellow, and turquoise enamel. 2" x 1-1/16". $25-35.

David Mandell
"The Show Must Go On"
1970s - 2002

David Mandell first made jewelry as a child. He loved to string beads. Since his father was a jewelry wholesaler, he had a firsthand opportunity to learn about the world of jewelry. By the 6th grade he was buying supplies from jewelry catalogs and his teachers became his best buyers. During this time the flea market trade was booming, David tried it and he didn't sell a piece of his jewelry.

David Mandell

During 1981-1983, he followed his artistic inclinations and went to the Trappagen School of Fashion in New York. There he studied the history of costume design, fashion design, and illustration and was awarded the Charles Revson Grant.

In the later 1980s he worked as an evening wear designer as well as an assistant wardrobe designer. He created jewelry for numerous movies and nurtured a desire to learn to make "show girl" jewelry. By the end of the 1980s, he tried jobs in the restaurant business, only to find he didn't like them as well as stringing beads. Mandell apprenticed with Lary Vrba and learned how to solder jewelry. There was no one better than Vrba. During this period, Mandell also designed floral and theatrical party designs for various corporate and residential clients in the New York metropolitan area.

When Mandell became aware that many people were collecting Christmas trees, he made them as "objects of art" to be enjoyed throughout the year. Sometimes he even created backgrounds for his pieces. "The Show Must Go On" trees all have a similar feeling, but are each slightly different. Mandell always uses one trembling present beneath each tree. The trees are usually plated in the 1940s-style of "dog plating." He likes to create striking pieces: sometimes in all blues, all reds, all jets, crystal and aurora borealis, or opaque stones such as matrix, peridots, and moonstones. His stones are hand faceted. David Mandell has now created several large light-up trees and one recent tree sports little pink plastic bells from the 1950s.

Mandell's signature color is orange, so many jewelry pieces have this color on it somewhere (see an example in the box below). Mandell's life has been intriguing and unusual. Is it any wonder that his jewelry follows the same path being creative, unusual, and dynamic?

"The Show Must Go On." A traditionally styled tree with a creative twist. This tree is so large it uses a three-inch pin on the back. The star, (5 gold balls and five amber navettes), at 2-1/2," along with a gift (in amber baguettes, a gold metal band which is tied with a gold cord) is 5/16" long. Both are connected to the tree by a coiled spring. Each separate piece has the designer's mark. The tree is made with dark green navettes (25), lighter green pears (23), and many differently sized and shaped dark green stones. Over them all is a swag of rhinestones. Pronged. 1999. 7-1/2" x 3-1/2". $300-350.

"The Show Must Go On." This is a wonderful tree of opaque, clear, and light green navettes and pear shapes. A rhinestone garland crisscrosses over the tree. The topper is a scalloped aurora borealis stone surrounded by smaller aurora borealis stones (12). Tiny round light green stones dot the edges. The stones are mounted on a platinum base. A present of clear rhinestones wrapped with an amethyst bow and silver ribbon trembles off the base of the tree. Pronged. 1999. 6-1/2" x 3-3/8". $300-350.

"The Show Must Go On." A beautiful tree by Mandell in two shades of opaque green navettes and emerald cut stones which are all prong set. The backing and prongs are in silver to keep the soft feeling of this tree. Light green clear stones in different sizes of pear shapes, an aurora borealis garland, and a flower-shaped star enhance the tree's color. Little pink plastic bells (out of the 1950s) hang from the tree. The top star and the packages are tremblers. The tree has a dimensional base, so it can be used as a sculpture as well as a pin. This is a wonderful piece. Pronged. 1999. 6-7/8" x 4-1/2". $300-350.

Marvella
1911-2002

A tree of pearls (10) graduated in size from the largest on the bottom to the top. The pearls are stacked with tiny gold balls between each one and a gold star is at the very top. 2" x 1-1/2". $35-45.

Mary O

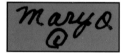

A tree made from wood covered with a plastic coating. Green and gold paint creates the design on the wood. Rhinestones are applied to the coating. 2-3/8" x 2-1/16". $5-10.

Mastercraft

Ten marquis stones are outlined by small green stones (10) and each tier is layered for added dimension. Red stones (12) accent the outside edges. It was designed by Patalli. 2" x 1-5/8". $65-80.

Bobbi Mathis
1998~2002

Bobbi Mathis

Bobbi Mathis received her BA in Art Education from Western Michigan University at Kalamazoo, Michigan. She enjoys creating pins for each season of the year. These trees are made from sculpy clay. Currently she is designing with stained glass. Signed: BM or BJM.

A rosette tree in pinks, purples, blues and gray. Clay. 2-3/4" x 1-1/2". $2-5.

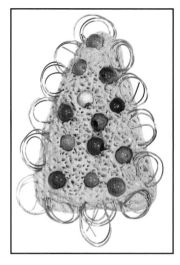

A snowy tree which looks like icing decorated with candy balls. Clay. 3-1/8" x 2-1/8". $2-5.

Hitachi Maxell, Ltd. Japan

This is a copy of Hillary Clinton's Christmas tree. It is gold tone with six flashing lights. Marked. 2" x 1-3/4". $50-65.

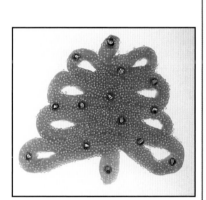

A tan pretzel tree with gold balls. Clay. 2-1/8" x 2-3/8". $2-5.

Tall slender tree with duck squawking out "Merry Christmas," Clay. 3-3/8" x 3/4". $2-5.

Tree strung with miniature light bulbs and colored ball. Clay. 3-1/8" x 1-7/8". $2-5.

Mel Lions

Mel Lions is an artist who lives in Connecticut. No longer doing Christmas pieces, she still likes to do Bakelite pieces and dangling vintage earrings. She sells on the internet.

This Mel Lions pin is fun to wear. It depicts things one might find on Christmas morning under the Christmas tree: a train, a tennis racket, a stocking, golf clubs in a bag, and a bird. The pin was made from bits and pieces of jewelry from different eras. The back of this pin is made from an old copper pin marked "MATISSE / RENOIR." 2-3/4" x 4-1/8". $90-125.

Merksamer

A three-dimensional tree whose branches point outward giving a realistic look. Tiny jewel-colored stones are sprinkled throughtout the tree. 1-7/8" x 1-1/4". $35-45.

Metzke

Here is a contemporary tree made from sterling silver. Each branch looks like a "W," or like a stylized crown. 1-3/4" x 1". $40-50.

Museum of Fine Arts, Boston

This is the Christmas pin offered by the Museum of Fine Arts of Boston. Every year they select items which represent the Christian and secular winter holiday season to be reproduced and offered for sale. Each piece is inspired by an art object in their collection.

"Adoration of the Magi." This Christmas pin was inspired by an oil on fabric painting by Bartholome Zeitblom (1455/60-1518/22). German. Marked: mfa.Boston. 1999. 2-1/4" x 1-1/2". $30-40.

Mimi di N
1962

Mimi di Niscemi is known for fantasy jewelry.

Here is an enameled snowman holding a tree and a cane . 2-1/2" x 1-5/8". $35-50.

M. J. ENT.

A tree with swooping rows of red, green and clear stones (35). Marked M. Jent. 2-1/4" x 2". $35-45.

Here is a copper doggie tree. The tree has a hound dog head, feet, and paws. A stocking hat sits on the dog's head with a candy cane dangling off its tip. It has a garland of rhinestones (13). Marked M Jent. 2" x 1-1/4". $25-35.

M. J. ENT. has created a modern tree from ten flowers in white enamel. In each center is an aurora borealis stone. The white enamel flows over the entire tree right down the stem into the pot. It is dynamic. Marked CMJ ent. 1999. 2-1/4" x 1-1/2". $25-35.

Monet 1937-2002

In 1937, two brothers, Jay and Michael Chernow, set up their own jewelry company in New York City. It has always been a giant in the jewelry business.

A zig-zag design set with graduated rhinestones. 2-3/4" x 1-3/8". $50-65.

A stylized tree in a ribbon design. Multi-colored stones (15) used.1998. 2-3/8" x 1-3/8". $40-55.

Modern Woman

A group of silver trees accented by a gold star. Marked TC, but on a Modern Woman card. 1999. 1-7/8" x 1-3/8". $10-15.

A round broach with green enameled trees and three rhinestones. 1998. 1-3/8" Diameter. $30-40.

A tree whose body is slightly rounded and covered with an opalescent glaze. Silver lines and a silver star add decoration. 1999. Marked on card only. 2-3/8" x 1-1/2". $10-15.

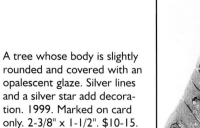

A white textured ribbon tree set with aurora borealis stones (12). 2-1/8" x 1-1/2". $30-40.

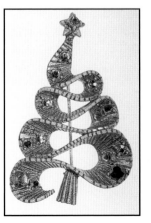

This is a small textured tree with multi-colored cabachons (9). 1/2" x 1". $25-35.

A small tree whose four tiers are layered and covered with stones (15). 2-1/8" x 1-1/4". $40-65.

Monet 2

The tree made entirely out of stacked green enameled triangles. Each triangle contains a single clear stone. 2001. 1-7/8" x 1-5/8". $15-20.

Here is a nicely tailored tree where the edge of the tree is repeated three more times for added dimension. The last repetition holds the only stone on the tree. 2001. 1-7/8" x 1-1/2". $15-20.

MONT

This is a pretty tree using pastel colored stones outlined in gold. 2001. 2-1/2" x 2". $25-35.

Jennifer Moore

This Jennifer Moore tree has diagonal tiers with colored stones (17). Cast pewter. Unsigned. 2-1/4" x 1-1/4". $35-45.

MV

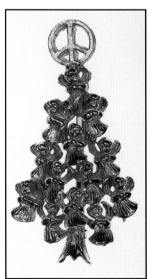

Two similar trees, one in silver and one in gold tone. The trees are stacked angels with a peace sign on top. The silver one has a green stone glued over the peace sign. Probably from the late 1960s. 2-3/4" x 1-3/8". $45-100 each.

Mylu
Late 1960s - Early 1970s

Mylu was a branch of Coro Jewelry that specialized in holiday designs around 1968.

This is one of the unusual designs Mylu created. Here chunky, pink art glass stones (5) are set among watermelon tourmaline prism stones (7). Hard to find. 2-3/4" x 1-5/8". $250-300.

Four similar trees with differently colored stones. The tree is created from stacking diamond shapes that are connected by red, lime, aurora borealis, and magenta stones (25). Five faceted stones dangle from the bottom of each tree. 2-7/8" x 1-5/8". $95-125 each.

A lovely, delicate tree with leaves set with tiny blue, green, and clear stones. 2-3/4" x 2-1/4". $55-85.

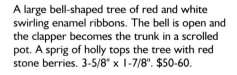

A large bell-shaped tree of red and white swirling enamel ribbons. The bell is open and the clapper becomes the trunk in a scrolled pot. A sprig of holly tops the tree with red stone berries. 3-5/8" x 1-7/8". $50-60.

Four tiers of fan styled branches which are layered to create this tree decorated with red dangling stones (7). 2-1/2" x 1-7/8". $60-70.

Two trees of the same lacy, floral design. One is flatter and enameled. Both have an ornate scrolled base. Unmarked. 2-1/2" x 1-5/8". $25-35.

Two bell-shaped trees in contemporary style. The seven primary stones of medium size are raised with a star impression in the metal. Left, gold tone, additional stones (20).Unmarked. 2-1/8" x 1-5/8". Right, silver tone stones (8). 2-1/2" x 1-1/2". $45-65 each.

The color here is rendered by colored stones (12). The tree is more rounded. Marked. 2-1/2" x 1-5/8". $50-65.

Three similar trees. A checkerboard design embellished with various finishes and differently colored stones (34). 2-7/8" x 1-5/8". $45-65 each.

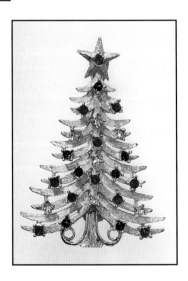

Tree of swooping branches covered with 3 colors of rhinestones (25). The trunk holds a gold baguette. 2-1/2" x 1-7/8". $50-65.

Similar design to the preceding but of brighter color. Tree trunk is not decorated. 2-1/2" x 1-7/8". $50-65.

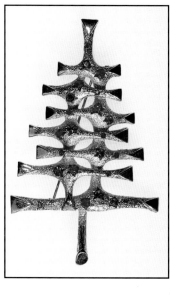

A wonderful abstract design that uses straight lines and open work. It is decorated with red and green stones (23). The metal is brushed gold while the edges of the branches are finished in polished metal. 3-1/2" x 2". $65-75.

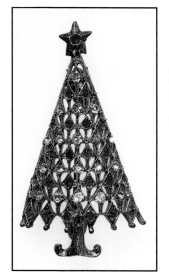

A stunning stacked-diamond design set with rows of red and clear stones (41). Bright green enamel is used to give pizzaz. 2-7/8" x 1-5/8". $60-75.

An old design used by Corel with five tiers of scalloped branches. The rhinestones between each branch look like a garland. Note the 10-pointed star. 2-7/8" x 1-3/4". $45-85.

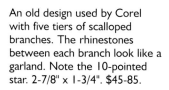

A tiny collar pin in silver with red and green stones. 1-3/8" x 1-1/8". $20-35.

This design has four tiers of branches and a rhinestone between each branch, with a 10-pointed star at the top. 2-1/2" x 1-1/2". $45-60.

According to Kathy Flood, this is the only unmarked Christmas tree designed by Marge Borofsky for Mylu. Gold fan branches are set with watermelon-colored stones (10). Tiny candles, with red stones, decorate the edge of each branch. Base broken off. 1-7/8" x 1-7/8". $130-175.

A tree in four tiers with edges scalloped in a rope design. Tiny multi-colored stones (24) decorate each level. 2-1/4" x 1-1/2". $50-60.

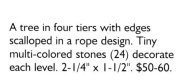

A gold lattice design set with alternating red and green stones (54). Star with a stone in each point and its center. Note the curly tree trunk. 2-3/4" x 1-1/2". $40-55.

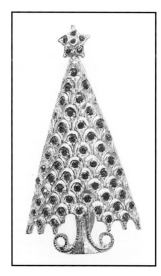

A brushed gold tree with scalloped tiers set with small red stones (10) and tiny clear rhinestones (9). Green metal dangles spell out "P-E-A-C-E". 2-7/8" x 2". $65-80.

A holly tree whose leaves are deep green enamel with clumps of dark red berries (13 stones). An ornate pot is used. 2-7/8" x 1-3/4". $35-65.

Similar trees, one in silver and one in gold, have branches with individual needles pointing downward. Tiny rhinestones top the branches (21). Tree pots appear wound with wire. 2-7/8" x 1-3/4". $45-85.

An unusual gingerbread cookie tree right out of "Hansel & Gretel." The pin is painted flat brown with a scroll design that looks like icing. 1-13/16" x 1-1/2". $50-125.

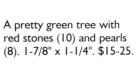

A pretty green tree with red stones (10) and pearls (8). 1-7/8" x 1-1/4". $15-25.

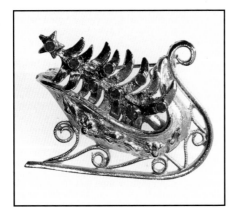

A goldtone sleigh bearing a tree in green wash dotted with red stones (8). 1-13/16" x 2". $30-45.

The gold Santa tree has two green eyes, a red nose, and a red stone in the star. 2-5/8" x 7/8". $50-75.

The simple outline of a tree with one red stone in the star. 3-1/4" x 2". $35-50.

Napier
1922 ~ 2002

The Napier company was founded in 1922 and has undergone many name changes. It is one of the oldest jewelry companies in the U.S.and still produces wonderful jewelry.

Two similar trees set with differently colored navettes. This one is slightly larger with darker colored stones. Pronged. 1-7/8" x 1-1/8". $50-75.

Pronged. 1-3/4" x 1-3/4". $50-75.

Two similar trees. This one has pearls and aurora borealis stones (17). 2" x 1-3/8". $45-65.

A filigree pin where pearls (10) are surrounded by a circle of rhinestones set in gold. A pear-shaped stone forms the top. 2-3/8" x 1-5/8". $35-55.

This one uses red and green stones (17). 2" x 1-3/8". $45-65.

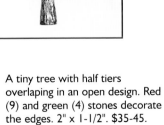

A tiny tree with half tiers overlaping in an open design. Red (9) and green (4) stones decorate the edges. 2" x 1-1/2". $35-45.

Two heavily textured trees of the same design, one in gold and one in silver. A star rests on top of each tree. 2" x 1-1/2". $25-35 each.

A small tree with milky white navettes (14) and rhinestones. This combination gives the pin a formal look. Pronged. 1-5/8" x 1-1/4". $45-65.

Nordstrom Stores

This Nordstrom pin is a tree with wonderful detailed needles. The gold accents set off the other colors. Little jewel-toned stones (8) are sprinkled throughout, with a red enamel bow near the top. 1999. 2-1/2" x 1-3/4". $85-100.

Oriental Trading Company

A pretty pin with tiny emerald stones in loops. A pear-shaped dangle hangs from each loop with two at the bottom. 4-1/2" x 2-3/4". $55-65.

Newpro

Stamped pin with red, green, and white enamel. Eight stacked Santas with tasseled hats. 2" x 1-1/2". $10-25.

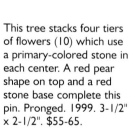

This tree stacks four tiers of flowers (10) which use a primary-colored stone in each center. A red pear shape on top and a red stone base complete this pin. Pronged. 1999. 3-1/2" x 2-1/2". $55-65.

Five trees with a snowman using red, green, and white enamel. 1-3/4" x 1-3/4". $10-25.

A design that is more fragile due to its open work. It has an outline of green navettes (11) clear baguette candles (2) and red and blue stones (4). Pronged. 1999. 2-1/2" x 1-1/2". $25-35.

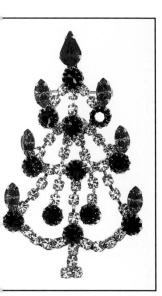

A gold tone tree with green stones (12) and amber navettes (6) with a pear-shaped stone on top. 2-7/8" x 1-5/8". $35-45.

Pakula

This company was founded in Chicago, Illinois, around 1940. Ads for this company's jewelry have been found for 1962 and 1963. Some think this company was connected in some way with the Hollycraft company, due to its similar designs.

A pin with primarily green navettes (17). Little primary-colored stones (12) tip one end of each navette. A single, clear, pear-shaped stone stands on top. Pronged. 1999. 3" x 2-1/2". $50-60.

Two wonderful candle trees that differ only in the color of stones used (17). Stones in graduated sizes decorate the long pointed branches. Clear baguette candles (7) with red enamel flames sit on the edges of the branches. This design is exactly like one used by Hollycraft. 2-1/4" x 1-3/4". $85-110 each.

A fragile looking tree outlined in clear stones and decorated with green round stones (17). 2-5/8" x 1-7/8". $35-45.

This design resembles flowers in full bloom using two colors of stones, in graduated sizes, as the centers. This one is old, but the design is being reproduced with indistnct marks. 2-1/4" x 1-1/2". $40-100.

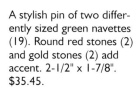

A stylish pin of two differently sized green navettes (19). Round red stones (2) and gold stones (2) add accent. 2-1/2" x 1-7/8". $35.45.

A tree decorated with cinnamon red bows, like the Hollycraft bowtie tree. Aurora borealis stones are used in the bows. 2-1/4" x 1-1/2". $45-60.

This double rope loop design includes medium sized stones (15) in two shades of green. 2-1/2" x 1-1/2". $45-110.

Similar to the preceding, but with multi-colored stones. The tree has a nice, lacy look. 2-1/2" x 1-1/2". $45-110.

A glitzy tree using chatons, baguettes, navettes, and a pear-shaped star. 2-5/8" x 1-7/8". $45-55.

Paquette

A simple cut-out tree in silver decorated with gold tone balls. The star and pot are also in gold tone. 2-1/2" x 1-3/4". $30-40.

A simple gold tone tree in four tiers with red and green stones (12) set into the brushed metal surface. 2-1/4" x 1-1/2". $40-50.

Jewels by Park Lane
1955-2002

Jewels by Park Lane, based in Schramberg, Illinois, distributes jewelry with a home party plan, much like the Sarah Coventry company. In 1955, Jewels by Park Lane was founded by Shirley and Arthur LeVin.

A silver bow tree in blue opalescent color. It has a ten pointed star without a stone. The Advertising Manager of Park Lane sent this to me as a gift for my collection. He thinks it is from the 1970s. A very pretty little tree. Unmarked. 2-1/2" x 1-1/2". $25-35.

Erwin Pearl
1970s ~ 2002

Erwin Pearl

Erwin Pearl started his career as an apprentice diamond cutter at the age of 16. He has won five Diamond International Awards and the Mikimoto Award for Innovative Pearl Design. He operates on the belief that "quality jewelry doesn't have to cost a fortune." In 1970, Pearl launched his fine fashion jewelry line. Some 30 years later, Pearl continues to bring beautiful, timeless, affordable jewelry to women the world over. *(Pearl, 2000)*

A wonderful tree of layered rhinestone branches. Red and green balls decorate each branch. It has a rooted trunk style. 1997. 2-1/2" x 1-15/16". $185-250.

Pell
1941 ~ 2002

The Gait Brothers founded this company in 1941 in New York. Today its headquarters are on Long Island. Many of the Pell pins feature long, slender baguettes.

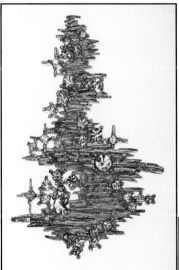

A most unusual abstract tree in deeply textured gold. Rhinestone balls (37) are clustered all over the tree. 1997. 2-1/4" x 1-1/2". $185-210.

The body of this tree has tiny green stones (37) and larger red and clear stones (9). Four baguette candles with red flames sit on the edges. 1-3/8" x 1-1/8". $95-125.

A beautiful gold three dimentional tree with silver balls dangling on the end of each branch. It also has a gold star with a stone on top. 1-7/8" x 1-1/2". $135-145.

This lovely old tree has four baguette candles with flames sitting on branches which are covered with clear, red, blue, and green stones. 2-3/16" x 1-1/2". $95-125.

This tree has five graduated tiers. Each tier has red and green round stones (14) and baguettes (13). A pear-shaped stone is on top. 2-1/2" x 1-3/4". $95-115.

Like the previous tree, but smaller, this one has fewer stones (10) in red and green, with a candle on each side. The tree has a large multi-faceted star on top. 2-1/2" x 1-1/2" $45-85.

This textured pin is cut out with three diagonal garlands, two of clear baguettes and one of red baguettes. Tiny colored stones are sprinkled over the tree. 2-1/8" x 1-7/8". $65-85.

A lovely tree with crisscrossing garlands of pavé rhinestones. Large ruby balls (5), emerald greens (2), navettes (2), plus small green stones (8) scallop the tree's bottom edge. 2-1/2" x 1-5/8. $65-110.

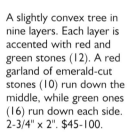

A slightly convex tree in nine layers. Each layer is accented with red and green stones (12). A red garland of emerald-cut stones (10) run down the middle, while green ones (16) run down each side. 2-3/4" x 2". $45-100.

Here is a wonderful angel tree. The stacked angels (10) have aurora boreal stones (13) in their gowns, a pearl face, and wings with aurora borealis stones (6). The bottom edge of the tree uses tiny pearls (20). 3-1/8" x 1-13/16". $65-80.

The five metal garlands drape down the gold tone tree. Nine layers of branches are accented with red, green, and blue stones. An unusual star is made of two stones. 2 -1/2" x 2". $45-100.

The next two trees are variations on the same design in which the inner section is pressed forward. This tree is more ornate with more stones (32). It also has a red baguette trunk and a single clear chaton on the bottom. 2-1/4" x 1-1/2". $25-75.

This pin has the traditional colors of Christmas—red, green, and clear—in tiny stones (21). It has a plain, straight trunk. 2-1/4" x 1-1/2". $25-75.

"The Birthstone Tree." The insert in the Pell box reads, "This uniquely collectible pin is 24K gold plated & handset with Swarovski jewels & faux pearls. It is especially redesigned by artist Mary Beth Burchardt-Bruder using its archive model from the 1940's by Pell Jewelry Co." 2000. 2-3/4" x 1-3/4". $90-125 each.

"The Twinkle Tree." An absolutely gorgeous tree which seems to twinkle with light. It uses emerald green crystals surrounded by the tiniest red, blue, and clear crystals plus pearls. If one looks carefully, where each candle projects upward, you see that the red candle base is the trunk of another tree. 2000. Designed by M. B. Burchardt-Bruder. 2-3/4" x 2-3/4". $100-150.

p. heck designs

The p. heck design studio is on the outskirts of Minneapolis, Minnesota. Each design is done by hand and no two pieces are alike.

A contemporary design in ceramics. The color is dark green sprinkled with glitter for balls. The star on top is layered in gold. This design is called "fir". 1999. 3-1/4" x 1-3/4". $25-35.

"The Snowberry Tree." Faux pearl flowers (11) are surrounded by red enamel beads (22) (snowberries). A cross in blue crystal stands on top of the tree. 2000. Designed by M. B. Burchardt-Bruder. 2-1/2" x 1-3/4" $90-125.

PIM

A charming PIM tree with two layers of branches. The color combination is striking, using olive enamel for the pine tree and magenta stones (14) for the balls. 1-15/16" x 1-1/2". $25-35.

Pauline Rader

Pauline Rader started her jewelry design business in 1962 for private clients and boutiques. Although assisted by her brother and sister-in- law, all the jewelry was signed "Pauline Radar." Pauline's father owned a jewelry store where she grew up learning to design and construct pearl pieces. She had an interest in antique jewelry and traveled throughout the world, especially Greece, Italy, and France, searching for old pieces to adapt to her own style. (Ball & Torem, 1996).

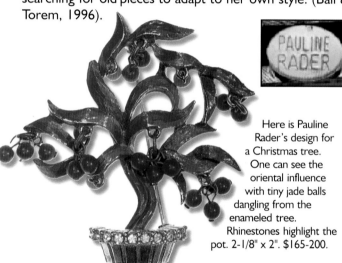

Here is Pauline Rader's design for a Christmas tree. One can see the oriental influence with tiny jade balls dangling from the enameled tree. Rhinestones highlight the pot. 2-1/8" x 2". $165-200.

Radko

A cute little pin with Santa and a tree. This pin came with a signed Radko ornament of the same design and an attached card reading "Radko." Unmarked. 2000. 2-7/8" x 1-3/4". $15-25.

Rafaelain

A little tree with two layers of branches, each layer a different shade of metal. Same style as Mylu trees. It has multi-colored stones (14). 1-7/8" x 1-3/8". $30-35.

Regency
1940s-1960s

No dates are available for Regency, but it resembles other jewelry made between 1940 and the early 1960s. Quality jewelry like this is collectible and hard to find.

This design is the only known Christmas tree pin made by Regency. The tree is an opencut design with three candles with flames. Various colored stones of different shapes and sizes are used in the body of the tree. The outline is a rope design. Pronged. 2-7/8" x 1-1/2". Unmarked $135-150. Marked $225-300.

Richelieu
1911 ~ 2002

A chunky gold tone tree with a pearl (15) garland and a star on top. Tiny rhinestones (6) sit on the edges of the tree. 1-7/8" x 1-1/2". $25-35.

Original by Robert
1960 ~ 1979

Robert Levy, David Jaffe, and Irving Landsman created the Fashioncraft Company in 1949. But when Landsman left the company in 1960, Levy and Jaffe changed the company name to Robert Originals, Inc. After Levy retired in 1975, David Jaffe's daughter Ellen, who was a designer for the company, became president and the company name was changed to Ellen Designs for Robert Originals. In 1984, the company name was changed to Ellen Designs, Inc. (Ball, 1997). All the trees shown here have plain pots, so the focus will be on the trees themselves.

A gold tone tree set with baguette candles in red and green. Rhinestones complete the decor. Marked and unmarked. 2-1/4" x 1-1/2'. $75-175.

Small goldtone tree, much like a Mylu design, with red and green stones. The pot, however, is all Robert. 2-1/2 x 1-3/4". $75-150.

Another foliage tree with a different leaf. This is a shorter bush with the same type of pot and the same pearl balls which dangle. 2-3/8" x 1-3/4". $150-175.

Here green enameled holly leaves are layered for depth. Small pearls (11) dangle from individual leaves. Rhinestones (11) are pronged. 2-5/8" x 1-7/8". $150-175.

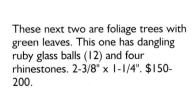

These next two are foliage trees with green leaves. This one has dangling ruby glass balls (12) and four rhinestones. 2-3/8" x 1-1/4". $150-200.

This tree, similar to the preceding one, has ten ruby balls and no rhinestones. 2-3/8" x 1-1/4". $150-200.

An entirely different style tree by Robert. This tree has a flat, dark green enamel with a garland of mutli-colored pastel enamel balls. It stands on a rounded base. 2-3/4" x 1-1/2". $90-125.

A dimensional tree with projecting branches. Red and green glass balls (8) dangle from the branches. Tiny red and green stones (17) decorate the spine of the tree. 1-1/2" x 1". $110-125.

Rodox

A gold Rodox tree, set in the center of an open square frame, has tiny enameled balls. 1-1/8" square. $15-35.

Rogers

The Kim Rogers pin is a red sleigh with a green enameled tree set with clear rhinestones. 1-7/8" x 1-1/2" $10-15.

Roma

A green enamel tree with red and white balls. 1-3/4" x 7/8" $40-50.

The small gold tree has red, green, and clear stones which provide its color. 1-5/8" x 1-1/8". $40-50.

Another small tree in green enamel. The only decoration is a garland of metal balls. A single clear stone is on top . 1-3/4" x 1-1/8". $40-50.

These two trees are enameled and have open stars in their bodies. Tiny colored stones (7) are sprinkled over the trees. Issued 1997. 1-1/2" x 1-1/4". $10-15 each.

Three trees using a wire pattern with three tiers of garlands in red and clear, red and green, and green and clear stones (23). Issued 1997. 1-3/4" x 1-1/4". $10-20 each.

Roman, Inc.
1965 ~ 2002

These trees are marked with paper tags. They were made in the Czech Republic.

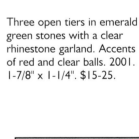

Three open tiers in emerald green stones with a clear rhinestone garland. Accents of red and clear balls. 2001. 1-7/8" x 1-1/4". $15-25.

Green navettes and red and clear balls create this tree. 1-3/4" x 1-1/2". $25-35.

Lines extend down from the top star to create this tree. Aurora borealis stones (23) sitting side-by-side form a solid top. More stones (11) are sprinkled over the rest of the tree. 1997. 2-1/2" x 1-3/8". $15-25.

Similar trees in design but with different metals, stone colors, and glitter. These are from Roman Inc.'s Wenceslaus Crowne Line. Marked only on their cards. 1999. 2-3/8" x 1-3/4". $25-35.

An Eisenberg-looking tree of clustered gold balls and rhinestone centers (10). 1997. 2" x 1-1/2". $10-15.

Rosa Designs

A glass tree outlined in silver with a silver garland. A colored stone brightens each section of the tree. Newport, N.Y. 2-1/4" x 1-3/8". $20-35.

A scroll design tree set with red, green, and blue stones (13). 1997. 2-1/8" x 1-5/8" $10-15.

Russ

The Russ trees are made of molded plastic. The backs are flat but the rest of the trees are three-dimensional.

A design similar to Hollycraft set with aurora borealis stones (23). Silver tone. 1997. 2-3/8" x 1-7/8". $10-15.

Snowman tree with a red hat. 1-1/2" x 1-3/8" $10-20.

Green tree with gold star. 2-3/8" x 1-5/8". $10-25. Mark: Russ China.

RVP

A small molded tree in four tiers, with four tiny stones. A squashed star with a single stone sits on top. Dangling from the bottom are a bicycle, a tie, and a ring. 2-5/8" x 1-1/4". $15-25.

Savvy Swarovski

This tree was made for the Savvy line of Swarovski Crystal in Austria. The tree has a paper tag with the Savvy logo.Unmarked. 1999. 2-1/8" x 1-1/2". $35-45.

Sheridan

An interesting sterling silver tree with deeply grooved horizontal branches. Six balls join the branches. 2-1/2" x 1-1/2". $50-65.

Siluane

This glittery tree has a background of clear rhinestones and multi-colored larger stones (18) in graduated sizes sprinkled over the tree. The trunk is made with red stones (6) and three green stones create the base. A red pear-shaped stone sits on top. Pronged. 2-3/4" x 1-3/4". $65-90.

S.F.J.

All three S.F.J. trees use crackle-green enamel.

A nice tailored design in three tiers with the edge of the first tier swooping downward embellished with gold balls and rhinestones (6). Each tier is edged in gold and the bottom tier has two more rhinestones. 2-1/4" x 1-5/8". $15-25 each.

A whimsical little tree which reads, "I love Christmas." Six stars with rhinestones hanging from the bottom. 2-1/2" x 2". $15-25.

A stylized tree using side curves, four arches with rhinestones (20), and cutouts. A red enamel star is added. 2-1/8" x 1-1/2". $15-25.

Silver Starrs

The 1999 Silver Starrs designs look much like the old Hollycraft designs. Marked on pin and a paper tag.

Vertical branches that are layered and set with ruby red stones (14). 1999. 2-3/8" x 1-7/8". $20-35.

This is a design often used by Kramer. It has six tiers in brushed gold highlighted with aurora borealis baguettes (24). 1998. 2-1/4" x 1-5/8". $35-45.

Groups of flowers with ruby red centers (13). Each flower has a half loop in a rope design underneath it. 1999. 2-1/4" x 1-1/2". $30-45.

A striking tree where textured rope branches fall downward with fuchsia and green aurora borealis stones between them. 1998. 2-1/4" x 1-1/2". $30-45.

Beautiful antique gray tree with silver trim plus large red stones (12) and star on top. 1999. 2-1/4" x 1-1/2". $20-35.

Swooping vertical branches set with ruby red stones (21) and silver balls. 2-1/2" x 1-3/4". $30-45.

Here are five overlapping tiers set with ruby stones (13). 1999. 2-1/2" x 1-3/8". $20-35.

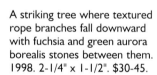
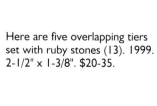

Beautifully designed tree.1999. 2-1/4" x 1-1/2". $30-45.

Holly leaf design. 1999. 2-3/8" x 1-7/8". $30-45.

Open design with pearls. 1999. 2-1/2" x 1-3/8". $30-45.

Open design with stones. 1999. 2-3/8" x 1-7/8". $30-45.

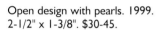

Gold tree with pearls. 1999. 2-3/8" x 1-7/8". $30-45.

Six tiers with stones. 1999. 2-3/8" x 1-1/2". $30-45.

Black tree with red stones.1999. 2-1/4" x 1-1/2". $30-45.

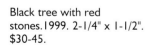

Bowtie tree with stones. 1999. 2-1/4" x 1-5/8". $30-45.

S.J.C.
1995 ~ 2002

Original S. J. C. cards read as follows:

> ORIGINAL COLLECTION By
> S. J. C.
> Hand crafted with highest quality materials
> New York Paris London Milan

These two trees are similar in design with different ornaments. The trees are made with a plastic covering which resembles green foil and a gold tone beaded garland which crisscrosses from top to bottom. Christmas tree balls and stars are randomly scattered. The tree with a present is from 1999. The tree with a toy soldier is from 1995. 3-1/4" x 1-3/4". $15-25 each.

Lou Slowek of Slowek Designs
1990 ~ 2002

Lou Slowek

"THE CURIOSITY SHOP INC." COLUMBUS, OHIO

Lou Slowek is already an established artist in watercolors and sketching with several Limited Editions to his credit. He has also designed "one of a kind" and "Limited Edition" jewelry for the general public.

For the past few years Lou has been concentrating on repair, restoration, and redesign of collectible costume jew-

elry. Until recently, his designs have been created on a "special request" basis only for clients in Italy, England, South America, and throughout the United States. Lou's new designs are on a very limited basis, since he makes each piece by hand whenever he has a break from the other parts of his business. With no plans or desire to go into mass production, there are a very limited number of pieces in existence and all are in private collections. It will be an exciting challenge for the collector to acquire one of Lou's pieces .

Here is a lovely tree with swooping branches done in a green wash. At the end of each branche is a gold star (8) set with a single rhinestone. One star is also on top. 2-1/8" x 1-3/4". $40-65.

This is a lacy and delicate tree constructed on metal arms with connectors. The design has six rhinestone flowers, each with clear rhinestones (12) and green cabochons (6) highlighted by graduated pearls and fine green, enameled metal needles. This pin could be worn at times other than Christmas. 6-1/2" x 4-1/2". $250-275.

Amanda Smith

AMANDA SMITH

An unmarked tree in a box marked Amanda Smith. A splashy contemporary tree with rows of alternating green (32) and clear (39) rhinestones. This design is a variation of a Monet design. 1998. 2-1/2" x 1-3/8". $25-35.

Stefanie Somers

Stefanie Somers is from Texas. This pin is from her Stefanie Somers Collection.

"Noel Tree." A delicate tree of Austrian lead crystal navettes (14) with ruby accents (12). Stones are glued to one another. Very fragile pin. 1997. 1-7/8" x 1-1/2". $40-50.

Spain

This lightweight pin has four tiers with a rounded body. It has the look of cloisonné using red, green, black, and white enamel in a decorative pattern. 2-1/4" x 1-5/8". $25-35.

Sphinx
1948 ~ 2002

Sphinx is a British company which started business in 1948. It produces jewelry for itself and other designers. They make quality pieces using Swarovski crystals. The maker's mark may not be readable. However, Sphinx uses a load number for identification.

Two similar trees designed with different decoration. Both have flowers of rhinestones and red faceted balls (17). This one has green enamel leaves. Load No. 1266. 2-5/8" x 1-7/16". $125-150.

This tree, similar to the preceding one, has gold leaves and three colors of faceted stones as Christmas balls. 2-5/8" x 1-7/16". $125-150.

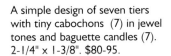

A simple design of seven tiers with tiny cabochons (7) in jewel tones and baguette candles (7). 2-1/4" x 1-3/8". $80-95.

A tree that looks similar to the two preceding pins, but this one is wider and more triangular in shape. Here, red round stones (17), with green enamel and rhinestone leaves, complete the design. The pot is brown enamel with gold edging and a gold bow. 2-5/8" x 2-1/8". $85-105.

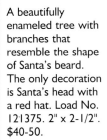

A beautifully enameled tree with branches that resemble the shape of Santa's beard. The only decoration is Santa's head with a red hat. Load No. 121375. 2" x 2-1/2". $40-50.

Spode

The Spode China Company of England has designed a Christmas pin as a miniature of its famous Christmas plates. It is made from Spode porcelain and features a Christmas tree. A fastener on the back enables it to be worn. It came in a box with red velvet paper and a clear plastic lid. This is a true collector's piece, especially for Spode lovers. 1-1/2" diameter. $50-75.

St. John

St. John jewelry is sold only at Jacobsons stores.

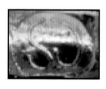

The simplicity and high quality of this tree make one stand back and admire it as a piece that would look great on anything. The opencut outline of branches in five tiers is decorated with two sizes of ruby stones. Pronged. 1999. 2-1/8" x 2". $95-125.

Rudolph the reindeer is pulling Santa's sleigh, connected by three chains. The colors are in enamel, except for Rudolph's red glass nose and two green stone eyes, and the tree's two tiny rhinestones. 1999. 3-3/4" x 1-5/8". $95-125.

St. Labré

A unique design, this tree has seven branches of green rhinestones (57), magenta balls (4), and clear baguette candles (4) with amber flames. Oval metal ornaments with a red center stone dangle from the front. A wonderful 12-prong star with a rhinestone sits at the top. The trunk is fan shaped. 1960s. Pronged. 2-1/2" x 1-7/8". $95-125.

Lea Stein of Paris

From the archives of Lea Stein-Paris comes this design from the 1960s which has never before been created, until now. Kathy Flood found it in the Stein archives and is the sole seller of it. The pin uses Stein's own lamination technique in cellulose acetate. It is three-dimensional in alternating layers of solid tortoise shell pattern and textured red. The star on top is made of red, blue, and amber. 2000. Colors available are: green, snow white, silver, blue, and orchard. Most interesting and exquisite. 3-1/2" x 2-1/8". $95-125.

Swarovski Crystal
1988 ~ 2002

Swarovski Crystal of Austria started using the swan logo in 1988. Each piece of jewelry is hand polished and hand set with Swarovski crystals. Their speciality lines are packaged in padded boxes to prevent scratches. Swarovski's Signature line is a middle-priced line. Some Swarovski trees came originally with paper identification tags.

A multitude of clear crystal navette and round stones, dotted with red stones in two sizes. Every stone is outlined in gold. A multi-stone star sits on top and the base has clear crystals. 2-5/8" x 1-5/8". $80-95.

A different look in the Limited Edition line. Here are four tiers of tiny green stones, with each tier outlined in clear crystals. Jewel colored stones (navettes and squares) sparkle between the green stones. A single baguette forms the tree's trunk. 2-3/8" x 1-1/2". $80-95.

A wonderful new "swan" sleigh from Swarovski. Look carefully and you'll see the sleigh is in the shape of a swan, which is the Swarovski logo. The sleigh's rudder also picks up the curve of the swan's neck. It is filled with tiny rhinestones, a green enamel tree, and one large ruby swan wing. An absolutely wonderful design. 2000. 3-1/2" x 2-1/2". $65-85.

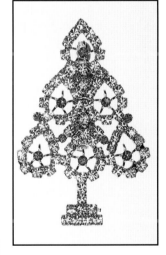

A delicate tree decorated with tiny blue stones and clear rhinestone loops. Paper tag marked. 2-1/2" x 1-5/8". $40-75.

A small convex tree made of clear crystals and round balls of red, green, and blue that sparkle on the tips of gold branches. Signature line. New in 1996. 1-7/8" x 1-1/4". $70-85.

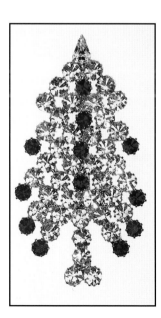

This crystal tree has branches which hang down with a red crystal ball (8) at each end. Four more red balls decorate the tree's spine. Pronged. 3-1/4" x 1-5/8". $50-90.

A stunning blue crystal tree with white milk glass details. Pronged. 3-1/8" x 2-1/16". $50-90.

Here is a combination of large clear navettes surrounded by clear pavé rhinestones. Red, blue, and green cabachons are sprinkled over the rest of the tree. Limited Edition. Sold in 1995 for $115. Hard to find. 2-3/4" x 2". $200-300.

The back side of the preceding pin. Notice the wonderful red enameling.

Rows of small stones are pavé-set in clear crystals with gold prongs and each row is slightly arched. The same angel top as the preceding but with a metal diamond shape behind it and outlined in crystals. 3-1/8" x 1-5/8". $50-65.

This tree has four layers of branches with pavé rhinestones dotted with red, blue, and green cabachons (9). Swarovski Jeweler's Collection. 1998. 2-1/4" x 1-1/4".Sold originally for $65. $80-100.

Rows of large clear crystals are pavé set straight across and with a gold garland. The top decoration is an outline of an angel with pink face, gold hair, and a metal halo. Pronged. 3-1/8" x 2". $50-65.

A contemporary design using clear (60), red (19), and green (3 large) chatons. There are also green baguette candles (4) and a pear-shaped star. Pronged. 2-3/4" x 1-3/4". $75-85.

Same style as the preceding except flat and accented by a gold garland and star. One large rhinestone sits at the base. Pavé rhinestones with tiny red, blue, and green stones (13) used as accents. Swarovski Jeweler's Collection. 1999. 1-3/4" x 1-1/8". Sold originally for $65. $80-100.

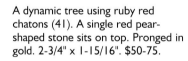

A dynamic tree using ruby red chatons (41). A single red pear-shaped stone sits on top. Pronged in gold. 2-3/4" x 1-15/16". $50-75.

Fuchsia stones with four gold angels and a top angel with clear crystals and a gold halo. Pronged. 3 1/2" x 2 3/4". $50-65.

Clear crystal chatons (38) create this tree which is swagged by a gold garland and has green baguette candles (6) and five additional stones. A star with a blue stone is on top. Pronged. 2-3/4" x 2-1/16". $65-80.

library. We would like to keep you informed about other publications from Schiffer Books.
Please return this card with your requests and comments.

Title of Book Purchased _____
☐ Purchased at: _____ ☐ received as a gift
Comments or ideas for books you would like to see us publish: _____
_____
_____

Your Name: _____
Address _____
City _____ State_____ Zip_____
E-mail Address _____

☐ Please send me a **free** Schiffer Antiques, Collectibles, Arts and Design Catalog
☐ Please send me a **free** Schiffer Woodcarving, Woodworking, and Crafts Catalog
☐ Please send me a **free** Schiffer Military, Aviation, and Automotive History Catalog
☐ Please send me a **free** Whitford Body, Mind, and Spirit Catalog
☐ Please send me information about new releases via email.
    We don't share our mailing list with anyone

See our most current books on the web at **www.schifferbooks.com**

Contact us at: Phone: 610-593-1777; Fax: 610-593-2002; or E-mail: schifferbk@aol.com
SCHIFFER BOOKS ARE CURRENTLY AVAILABLE FROM YOUR BOOKSELLER

K: user\do\wp\basic\bouceback

SCHIFFER PUBLISHING LTD
4880 LOWER VALLEY ROAD
ATGLEN, PA 19310-9717 USA

PLACE
STAMP
HERE

The following four pins are similar in style but with different color combinations which affect their personal appeal. The first two pins have more pizzazz, but the next two are stunning in their simplicity of color.

In the first, clear chatons (60) form the background of this tree with large (9) and small ruby red chatons (2). There are also baguettes along the edge (6), a large red chaton for the trunk, and a pear shape on top. This design was also used by Eisenberg, Warner, and Weiss. Pronged. 2-1/2" x 1-3/4". $45-65.

A crystal tree in four tiers highlighted with multi-colored navettes. It is off set by a polished gold garland and tree trunk. 2000. 2-5/8" x 1-7/8". $125-150.

Similar design to the preceding but with a change of colors. 2-1/2" x 1-3/4". $45-65.

Another crystal tree with open branches decorated with cabochons (9) and candles (3) with amber flames. 2000. 2-1/4" x 1-1/2". $100-125.

Clear crystals pronged in silver. 2-1/2" x 1-3/4". $45-65.

Open branches are filled with clear, red, and green crystals. The tree rests in a crystal pot. 2000. 1-7/8" x 1-1/2". $65-85.

Although this pin appears to be all in light pink crystals, the pin uses a combination of pink and clear stones. Pronged in silver. 2-1/2" x 1-3/4". $65-110.

Four tiers of tiny colored stones are outlined with a clear crystal garland. 2000. 1-7/8" x 1-1/2". $65-85.

Tiny crystal tree with a green garland and tiny cabachon stones. 2000. 1-7/8" x 1-1/8". $65-85.

This elegant tree is part of the Swan Collection. The branches all are filled with Swarovski crystals in silver. 2000. 1-7/8" x 1-1/4". $85-95.

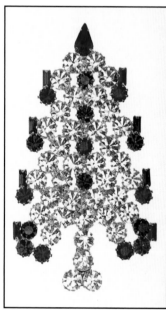
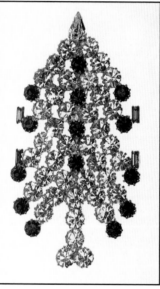

Blue-green stones (16) surrounded by rhinestones (36) create a pin with lots of pizzazz. Pronged. 1999. 2-1/2" x 1-3/4". $45-60.

Two similar trees with differently colored ornamentation and candles without flames. Notice the pear shaped stones used for the tops of the trees. Pronged. 3-1/4" x 1-3/4". $60-90 each.

Another candle tree in triangular shape with six red candles with amber flames and a blue star on top. Pronged. 2-5/8" x 2-1/4". $60-90.

Two trees that are similar in design but different in the colors of the metal. They both have an angel on top. In one, clear crystals and amber baguettes (10) are pronged in silver and used with a silver angel. In the other, a gold angel is on top and the stones are pronged in gold. 3-1/8" x 2". $45-55 each.

A crystal tree which is unusual with its springy candles (4). Notice the large crystal star on top. Pronged. 3-3/8" x 1-5/8". $50-90.

A beautiful Limited Edition piece with navettes (10) in an unusual cut encased in gold. Tiny clear stones surround everything. Enameled on the back. Sold in 1996 for $125. 2-1/8" x 1-3/8". $175-200.

An opencut tree in half tiers. The tree is set with rhinestones (84) and accented with amber stones (9). A large pear-shaped stone sits on top. Pronged. 1999. 2-3/8" x 1-5/8". $50-65.

A wonderful tree in three open tiers with a rhinestone garland at the bottom of each tier. Rhinestones are also used for the trunk and in the star. Two sizes of oval and round stones in red, green, and purple decorate each tier. 2-1/4" x 1-1/2". $75-90.

The back side of the preceding pin. Notice the wonderful red enameling and the swan mark.

This tree was made for the Savvy line of Swarovski Crystal of Austria. Unmarked. 1999. Tree has paper tag with Savvy logo. 2" x 1-1/2". $35-45.

Sweet Romance

A slightly convex tree of jewel-tone stones in three sizes. Among the jewels are four protruding balls, each made with six clear tiny rhinestones. 2-1/4" x 1-3/4". New in 1998 for $75. $85-100.

Black open metal design, one with dark jewel-tone stones (20) and the other with pastel tones (20). Bases have a square-cut stone in each pot. Sold on the internet. 2-3/4" x 2". $40-65 each.

Swoboda, Inc.
1950s-2002

This company produced jewelry in the early 1960s under the name Swoboda of California. It was well known for its useof semi-precious stones in heavy plated white metal. Nate Waxman, a former manager of Swoboda, is currently designing trees for the company.

A small, flat tree with round balls (10) of various sizes and colors. The colors used are unusual for the holiday season, but are typical of stones used on Swoboda jewelry. 1-1/2" x 1-1/8". $40-65.

This tree is made of asymmetrical pink stones and round garnet balls (10) with a larger ball on top. 2-1/4" x 1-3/4". $60-75.

A tree of half tiers, some in shiny gold and others in brushed gold, with colorful enameled balls. 1" x 1-1/2". $10-20.

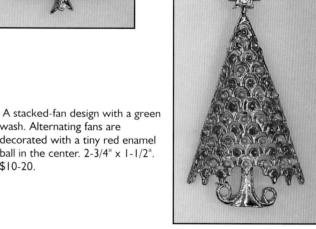

A stacked-fan design with a green wash. Alternating fans are decorated with a tiny red enamel ball in the center. 2-3/4" x 1-1/2". $10-20.

Tammey Jewels

The clear stones (9) used on this tree have a splash of white in them. In the middle of the tree is a crystal angel. 2000. 2-1/4" x 2". $25-35.

Taiwan

A tree using cut-out designs with variouslu colored enameled balls. 2-5/8" x 1-1/2". $15-25.

Tancer-II

Tancer-II was a division of Coro jewelry which was founded by Michael Tancer and two sisters, who originally worked for and founded Mylu.

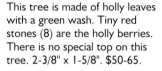

This tree is made of holly leaves with a green wash. Tiny red stones (8) are the holly berries. There is no special top on this tree. 2-3/8" x 1-5/8". $50-65.

A beautiful gold reindeer head tree with a blue star dangling from his antlers. It features a green navette eye. Mid-1970s. 2-7/8" x 1-1/2". $35-55.

A tall tree with layered holly leaves. Colored stones ((16) are scattered over the tree. The pot also has an open design. 3-1/4" x 1-3/4". $35-55.

A large reindeer's head has antlers with dangling irridescent balls (4) and a star.. It is designed exactly like the Mylu reindeer and comes unmarked. It features a red cabachon nose, a red navette eye, and a garland of holly. Mid-1970s. 3-1/8" x 1 5/8". $65-80.

Three tiers of red poinsettias alternate with four tiers of green leaves. Tiny aurora borealis stones (15) are scattered over the tree. Notice the star on top. 2-1/2" x 1-3/4". $35-50.

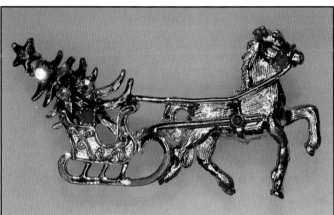

A horse and sleigh carrying a green-washed tree with colored stones (4). The horse sports a green eye. Mid-1970s. 2-7/8" x 1-1/4". $25-35.

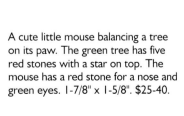

A cute little mouse balancing a tree on its paw. The green tree has five red stones with a star on top. The mouse has a red stone for a nose and green eyes. 1-7/8" x 1-5/8". $25-40.

A simple gold tone tree with five tiers of grooved limbs. Colored stones (18) cover the tree. 2-5/8" x 1-5/8". $20-35.

The six following trees all feature diamond patterns in an open design. Some of the trees have a trunk that turn up at the base. This one has scattered stones (9) and gold balls in its design. 2-3/8" x 1-1/4". $50-65.

An interesting tree created of crossed rope loops. Multi-colored stones (13) are scattered over the loops. The trunk is set in a large and ornate pot. 3-1/8" x 1-3/4". $50-65.

Stacked diamonds with five red and green stones that hang from the bottom of the tree. 2-7/8" x 1-3/8". $35-45.

Two similar trees except for their metal colors. The trees are made from (13) poinsettia flowers stacked in a rectangular shape. Each center holds a red stone. 2-3/4" x 1-3/8". $45-65 each.

This tree has a design similar to the two preceding trees, except it has dark red poinsettia flowers with green stone centers. The pot is slightly smaller than the others shown here. Unmarked. 2-1/2" x 1-1/2". $25-35.

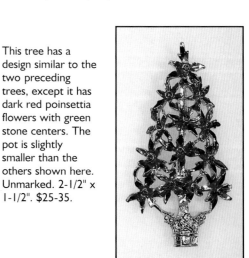

Four trees similar in design but with various colors of metal and stones. Unsigned. 2-3/4" x 1-3/4". $35-55 each.

Shown here is the most unique pin in this collection because it includes mink fur. It probably dates from the 1960s or 1970s when fur was considered an acceptable fashion accessory. 2-1/2" x 1-5/8". $130-150.

This tree has branches with needles in an open design. Red baguette candles (11) sit on the branches. A multi-pointed star is on top with a red stone. 2-3/4" x 1-7/8". $35-45.

A design, used often by Tancer, with individual branches swooping out to the sides. The trunk is ornate and ends in a complete circle. It has blue, green, and aurora borealis stones (23). 2-1/2" x 1-7/8". $50-65.

This shiny tree uses stacked squares joined by aurora borealis stones (10) and molded gold poinsettas (7). 2-3/4" x 1-1/2". $35-45.

Four cut-out branches with long needles. It is highlighted with green navettes (6). 2-1/4" x 1-1/2". $35-45.

Two trees similar to the preceding one but using differently colored stones (23). 2-1/2" x 1-7/8". $50-65 each.

Three tiers of layered branches that are shaped like fans. Red and green stones (12) decorate the tree. 2-1/4" x 1-5/8". $35-45.

This is a Mack bulldog, mascot of the Mack trucking company, which came with the tree with yellow stones. $55-70.

Here are two poinsettia trees. One has a pink wash while the other uses a red wash on the flowers. A tiny green stone (10) or a metal ball is the center of each flower. 2-1/2" x 1-1/2". $45-55 each.

A most unusual tree with dangling red and green navettes (10). Red and green enamel is applied along the tree's frame and trunk. 2-3/4" x 1-5/8". $60-85.

A small open tree which is decorated with tiny colored stones (7). 2-1/2" x 1-1/8". $30-45.

A different little tree with cut-out stars on each tier. The stars are in different sizes and have a tiny red, green, or clear stones (7) in the center of each. Several more stones are sprinkled here and there. This trunk is cut off at an angle. 2-1/4" x 1-3/8". $35-45.

Two trees which are similarly styled with dimensional branches and traditional holiday colored red, green, and clear stones (16). One rests in a pot and the other ends in a bare trunk. 2-1/2" x 1-1/2". $35-55 each.

Tara

A Santa head whose hat is a tree. Santa's beard and moustache are white enamel. The tree has colored stones (9) with a large star of aurora borealis at the top. 2-1/2" x 1-1/8". $55-70.

Another different Santa head whose hat is a tree. Santa's face and beard are gold. The tree has colored stones (7) with a large star of aurora borealis at the top. 2-1/8" x 1-3/8". $55-70.

A great gold outlined tree with "joy" written in bright green enamel across the center. The tree has a gold star on the top. c. 1940s. 1-3/8" x 1-3/4" $25-35.

Taxico

This silver tree is marked Taxico. It has Christmas balls of colored enamel. 2-1/8" x 1-1/2". $35-50.

This cut-out tree has a silver frame. Its top is set with a single rhinestone. 1999. 1-3/8" x 1-1/16". $10-20.

TC

Four tiers of dark green enamel with tiny enamel balls. 1999. 2-1/8" x 1-3/8". $10-20.

Here are green enameled holly leaves and red stone berries (6) decorating a tree of silver. 1999. 2-1/2" x 1-3/4 ". $10-20.

A tailored forest of silver with gold lettering,"all is calm, all is bright." One star dangles from the bottom edge. 1999. 1-1/16" x 2-1/8". $10-20.

An outline of a tree in opencut design. The bottom edge and sides are set with rhinestones. 1999. 2-3/8" x 1-3/8". $10-20.

A single tree in an open-cut design. The bottom edge is set with rhinestones. 1999. 2-3/8"-1-3/8". $10-20.

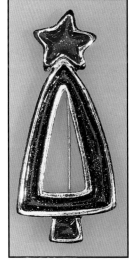

A triangular, open cut tree made with green and red sparkly enamel on a blue enameled base. 1999. 2-3/8" x 1-1/8". $10-20.

Teresa

Teresa Goodall lives in Minneapolis, Minnesota.

This tree is made from stoneware with olive green and white glaze. It is imprinted with a textured pattern. Glass beads of red and green are strung as a garland on a leather thong. The tree is marked and comes with a paper tag. 1999. 2-5/8" x 1-5/8". $35-45.

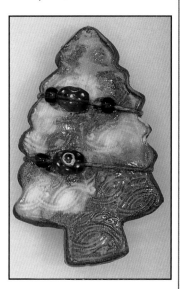

11 W. 30 St. Inc.

A little gold tree with sculptured stones (12) mounted on a silvertone metal base. Matching earrings, not shown. 1960s. Marked. 2-3/4" x 2-1/4". $35-45.

Tip Toe

A pair of most unusual trees; they are decorations for your shoes. The trees bend forward in the middle so that when they are attached to the front of a shoe, they stand up straight. The trees are goldtone in four tiers and sprinkled with multi-colored stones. 2-3/4" x 2-1/4". $35-45 the pair.

TOFA

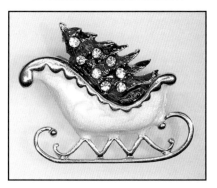

A red and green enameled tree on a white enameled sleigh. The pin is unmarked but comes on a TOFA card. 1-3/8" x 1-3/4" $10-20.

Torino, House of Eisenstadt

Pewter Christmas tree-shaped box with a lid which holds two small trees. The two trees can be worn as pierced earrings. The box holds a tree pendant charm of the same design with a chain. Box 1-3/4" x 1-3/8". $35-50 the set.

A pewter tree made of inverted fan designs. Tiny stones (19) sit on the fans. 2-1/8" x 1-3/4". $35-50.

Tortolani
1960-1975

This beautiful design is based on a candlestick decorated with pine tree boughs, an acorn, a star, and a bell. The branches are brushed gold with red and green rhinestone balls. 2-1/2" x 1-1/2". $45-65.

Trifari
1950s -2002

Gustavo Trifari Sr. and Leo Krussaman founded this company in 1918 as the Trifari & Krussman Company. Their Christmas line started in the 1950s, with this mark being used about 1954.

Four tiers of open limbs create this tree. The edge of each branch is beaded with clear stones for decoration. 2-1/4" x 1-5/8". $60-75.

Four tiers of tree limbs decorated with clear stones. 2-1/4" x 1-5/8". $95-125.

Two similar trees except one has jewels (13) and the other is plain. The four tiers of branches are brushed gold. 2-1/16" x 1-1/2". $65-100 each.

Two Sisters

The accompanying card to this jewelry reads, "Two Sisters/Medici Lauren and Leah." The sisters were inspired by ancient civilizations and blend their ideas into their designs. This jewelry is sold through the J.C. Penny Company.

This tree is small and all the detail is molded in the metal. Color is furnished by four stones. Unmarked except for the card. 1999. 1-1/2" x 1-1/4". $25-35.

A small lapel tree enameled green with irregularly shaped colored balls. The trunk is unusual in that it is concave. 1-3/8" x 1-1/8". $15-25.

Ultra Craft

A floral design similar to one shown in the Mylu section. It has clear stones (10) and scrolls. Pewter. 2-3/8" x 1-3/4". $25-35.

A gold tone tree with balls and flowers. Several flowers have stone (14) centers. 1-5/8" x 1-1/2". $30-40.

Van Dell
1938-2000

The Van Dell Company is from Providence, Rhode Island. Their jewelry designs often copied those of fine jewelry pieces.

This lovely tree has green enameled leaves mixed with five red and six clear rhinestone berries. 2-1/8" x 1-3/8". $50-70.

Vendome

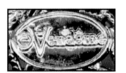

A tree with lots of sparkle from an openwork star and rows of trailing rhinestones and gold stars. At the top is a rhinestone angel. 1950s. 3" x 1-3/4". $25-35.

Vermont

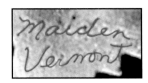

A tiny lapel pin made of pewter in the shape of a Christmas tree. It is molded with a flat back and the body has a crisscrossing garland, balls, and branches. Lots of detail for such a tiny pin. 1968. 7/8" x 3/4". $25-35.

Vero

Three enameled angels in a triangular design. The top angel holds a star and the bottom angels hold a wreath. 2000. 2-1/8" x 1-1/2". $20-30.

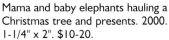

Mama and baby elephants hauling a Christmas tree and presents. 2000. 1-1/4" x 2". $10-20.

A "Merry Christmas" tractor-trailer truck with a green enameled Christmas tree on top of the cab and rhinestone hub caps. 2000. 2-1/4" x 1-1/4". $10-20.

Two deer stand next to a Christmas tree. 2000. 1-3/4" x 1-1/2". $10-20.

Bettina von Walhof
1980 - 2002

A spiral tree of textured gold. Tiny multi-colored stones dot the tree with green enamel edges. 2000. 1-3/8" x 2-1/2". $20-35.

Bettina von Walhof began her acting career at the age of four doing commercials. Her parents were animal trainers, so it was natural for her to star with them in the circus arena at the age of six.

She began a career as an animal trainer and performer in Germany. She worked with Johnny Weissmuller and performed all over Europe with her animals. She has trained gorillas, jaguars, leopards, cats, chimps, macaws, parrots, an alligator, and a boa constrictor. Many of her animals, as well as Bettina, have starred in television shows and movies with Marilyn Monroe, Jayne Mansfield, Bobbi Darrin, Paul Anka, and the Beatles. Due to her love of animals, she is an avid animal activist.

Today she and her husband travel between their homes in New York and Sarasota, Florida. However, they have just recently bought a villa in France where they will be growing grapes to make a white organic wine. Wherever they go, their pets go with them: a Cargo yellow finch, cats, two rats, two African lizards, a tarantula, and Mr. Baxter a Welsh Corgi.

Bettina has been in the jewelry and antique business for 30 years. She has been a dealer and collector since 1965. In the 1980s, she began creating her own pieces of jewelry. Her line of jewelry can be anything (especially all kinds and sizes of bugs and animals) which are a reminder of her past in the circus. However, she also creates holiday pieces, such as Christmas pins, Easter rabbits, and Halloween pumpkins. There are parrots, Buddhas, spiritual pieces, cartoon characters, designer dinnerware, candlesticks, and much more.

If you name it, she has probably done it, or at least tried it. Personalities such as Madeleine Albright, Hillary Clinton, and the members of the royal families in Europe all wear her jewelry. Her pieces are featured in the Ritz-Carlton Hotels, Jacobsen stores, and stores in Germany and Japan.

Bettina is now in the process of creating a Costume Jewelry Museum in New York or Sarasota, Florida. Everything has fallen into place except the "right" building. Her personal collection is some 7,000 pieces, and the museum will also feature other collections. Part of the monies from this museum will help sponsor a place for young people interested in jewelry design.

The *Herald Tribune Magazine* (Sarasota) named Bettina the "2001 Style Setter of the Year!"

"Blue Ribbon Tree." This stunning combination of clear and azure blue rhinestones, in round and emerald cuts, make an elegant pin. The ribbon is a trembler. The star projects beyond the front of the tree. 5" x 2-7/8". $165-250.

"The Russian Christmas Tree." An absolutely stunning piece that looks antique. There are two layers of branches. The upper tier is set forward for dimension and has rope-edged branches set with chunky rhinestones. The tree is accented with clear, emerald green, and ruby red stones. Hanging from the bottom branches are four rhinestone hearts enclosing a single red or green stone. 1999. 5-7/8" x 4-1/4". $200-265.

"Victorian Christmas Tree." This tree is made entirely with amber, clear, and two shades of green navettes. A garland of red and clear rhinestones crosses the tree. Tiny colored angels (4) and presents (3) decorate this tree. One larger angel sits on top. Pronged. 2000. 4-5/8" x 3-3/8". $200-265.

This tree that was a joint effort of Bettina von Walhof and Larry Vrba. Thus there are two name plates on the back of the pin. 1999. 3-3/8" x 3-3/4". $125-150.

Larry Vrba
1979 ~ 2002

Larry Vrba's pieces are bold and colorful. They are worn by those who want to be noticed for wearing something different. Lawrence (Larry) Vrba was born in Nebraska and is one of six children. During his formal schooling he was interested in music, drawing, and painting but he studied journalism. After militay service, he went to New York and worked in a wonderful fashion store "learning the ropes of high fashion, so to speak" from a display director. Vrba had always wanted to make jewelry so he worked for Miriam Haskell and became her head designer in 1969, and again from 1972-1978. He also designed for William deLillo very briefly in 1970, for Castlecliff from 1970 to 1972, and for Les Bernard. Vrba has designed for the New York Metropolitan Opera Company, the New York City Rockettes, Broadway shows, the Ringling Brothers Circus, fashion shows, movies, socialites, cross-dressers, etc. Vrba has designed pieces for Carol Channing, Liza Minelli, Debbie Reynolds, Jesse Norman, Joan Sutherland, Uma Thurman, Bette Midler, Patrick Swazee, and many more. Larry feels that designing Christmas tree pins is a natural category which he enjoys. Larry Vrba's pieces are bold, colorful, and wonderful.

A dazzler from the Fall of 1999. Six large emerald green round stones are surrounded by small light green chatons to create six sparkling flowers. Three clear baguette candles with large square amber flames sit away (3/8") from the tree. Red triangular faceted stones hang away from the tree. A huge star at the top has five clear lozenge-shaped stones. Notice the large purple trapezoid stone cut for the trunk. The body of this tree is arched and fairly heavy. Pronged. 3-5/8" x 3-1/16". $300-350.

Large emerald navettes patially outlined in rhinestones create the branches of this tree. Between the branches are single square ruby stones which become a garland. The trunk is made with clear rhinestones of different sizes and shapes. A magnificent star of large stones rests on top. 2000. Pronged. 4-1/2" x 2-1/2". $165-225.

This was a new tree for the Fall of 1999. It has a gunmetal frame and backing filled with stones of different shapes and colors. Three clear baguette candles with amber flames jut away from the tree. Large star on top. Pronged. 4-3/16" x 2". $165-200.

Here are five huge green oval faceted stones surrounded by small green chatons (60). Red chatons (10) decorate the tree and the base (16). A huge gold star is filled with clear rhinestones. Pronged. 1998. 3-3/4" x 2-1/4". $135-200.

This tree has the wonderful color combination of greens, purples, and blues accented by clear rhinestones and amber candle flames. It sits on a large blue stone with green and clear stone base and a single ruby stone which picks up the color of the candles. 1999. Pronged. 3-7/8" x 2-5/8". $250-350.

And the balls go round and round as they spin. The tree has six faceted twirling green beads in green rhinestone rings accented by three ruby red candles with amber flames. Sparkle is added by clear rhinestones. One tiny blue stone sits in the base. How wonderful and unusual. Pronged. 5" x 4". $250-400.

Here Vrba has used old cameo stones from Netti Rosenstein from the 1950s to create this tree. It is outlined in clear rhinestones and accented with clear baguette candles with dark blue flames. This pin is also found with pale pink Rosenstein cameos. 2000. Pronged. 5-1/4" x 3". $225-300.

Here each branch is like a fan spreading gold needles. Large dark green navettes are surrounded by emerald green chatons which are pronged in gold. Three clear candles with gold flames sit in front of the tree. The star on top is double layered with a 10-pointed, gold, solid background and a cluster in front. 2001. 4-15/16" x 3". $250-375.

A tree of frosty blue rectangles (12) accented with large dark blue faceted stones (8) on the edges. Three candles of clear baguettess have dark blue flames outlined in clear chatons. Large clear rhinestones create the trunk and the large star on top. This design is different and wonderful. It comes in this size and a few larger. 4" x 2-5/8". $165-190.

Here is a most unusual pin which looks as though it might have been made in the 1940s or '50s. The tree is made of six round pink plaques which look like pillbox hats. They are each topped with an aurora borealis flower (called a rose monteé) with a green chaton center. All the other stones are clear and arranged as three candles, a star, and a base. Very delicate looking, this pin is set in gold metal. Pronged. 2000. Limited Edition of 50. 4" x 2-15/16". $250-300.

Warner
1960 - late 1970s

Joseph Warner founded his company during the "Golden Age of Design," 1930s-1970s.(*Ball, 1990, 1997.*) Many of Warner's designs use black backing, a process known as "japanned."

The triangular shape of this tree is outlined in gold lines supporting red, blue and green stones (29). Under the base are four enameled gifts wrapped with gold cord. Two green baguette candles have clear flames. Pronged. 2-1/8" x 1-1/4". $85-125.

This tree is styled similarly to the preceding one except that garlands on the base have red and green stones (40). One emerald green stone creates the base. Pronged. 2-3/8" x 1-1/2". $75-125.

A wonderful design used by Warner, Weiss and Eisenberg Ice. The following two Warner trees (one large and one small) have many similarly arranged colored stones in different sizes. Four clear baguette candles are on the branch edges. This is a beautiful tree worth copying. Pronged. 2-1/2" x 1-5/8". $125-175.

Similar to the preceding tree but smaller. 1-15/16" x 1-1/8'. $65-95.

Watta

A cute little tree of resin on metal. A sock, sled, jack-in-the-box, bear, glass heart, toy drum, and present hang from the bottom. 3-7/8" x 1-1/2". $20-30.

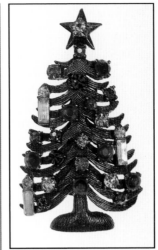

This metal tree is darker than the previous pin and the branches are layered with multi-colored crystals (21). White baguette candles (3) sit on top of the branches. 2-1/2" x 1-3/8". $125-165.

A tree similar to the two preceding but unmarked. 2-1/2" x 2". $90-125.

Weiss
1942 - Early 1970s

Albert Weiss, a former employee of Coro, founded his company in 1942. Weiss made costume jewelry using Austrian rhinestones. This jewelry is often compared to Eisenberg jewelry. It's heyday was the 1950s and 1960s.

Here is the original Weiss tree design that is highly sought by collectors. This design was also used by Warner, then almost exactly by Eisenberg Ice. Also found unmarked. 2-3/8" x 1-5/8". $125-150.

Two Victorian styled trees by Weiss. A metal tree which is deeply textured with swooping branches has multi-colored crystals decorating the spine (6) and branches (17). There are milky white baguette candles (7) with amber stone flames. 2-3/4" x 2-1/4". $175-235.

This Eisenberg Ice tree is almost identical to the Weiss design except for the trunk and the candles. One must look closely to see the difference. 2-3/8" x 1-5/8". $95-150.

An opencut design with red and green cabochons (9). The tree's base is one used often by Weiss. 2-3/8" x 1-3/4". $100-150.

Similar to the preceding tree but newer and with a gold finish. The S-scroll cutouts are larger and the round faceted stones are glued in place. 2-1/4" x 1-3/4". $185-250.

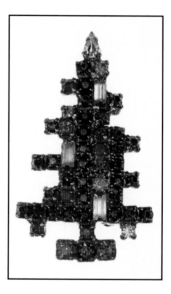

Here is probably the best known, and most highly sought after, Weiss Christmas tree pin. The following three trees could be called "The Weiss Trio" because the design comes in three sizes. A wonderful design with green stones (47) creating their own tiers. It is decorated with white baguette candles with gold flames (5). A clear pear-shaped stone sits on top. Other sizes and colors of chatons, plus another pear-shaped stone on the large tree, make this tree complete. The base is a horizontal row of amber stones (5) imitating the same line of the tree tiers. This, the smallest tree, has slightly darker green stones. 1-7/8" x 1-1/8". $150-185.

Here is an old tree in dark silver colored metal with an arched bottom which is longer on the left side. The tree has a rope garland criss-crossing its five tiers. There are scrolled S-cutouts between the iridescent stones (15). The stones are faceted in floral shape with clustered centers. They are attached with pronged pins. Notice the arc base. 2-1/4" x 1-3/4". $185-250.

Weiss made this tree design with matching earrings, a tie-tack, cuff-links, and scatter pins. These items are even harder to find than the trees. The scatter pins are unmarked. 1-1/4" x 7/8". Pair of scatter pins as a set $100-150.

2-1/2" x 1-3/8". $165-225.

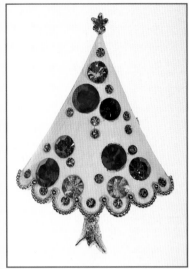

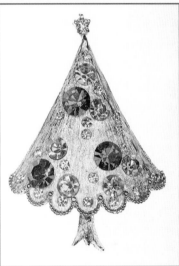

Two trees using the same design with a different color treatment. One has white enamel set with primary colored stones in three different sizes (27). The other is a brushed gold using two shades of green stones along with small clear stones. The bottom of the tree is a scalloped edge in a rope design. Excellent quality. 2-5/8" x 1-7/8". $85-110 each.

2-3/4" x 1-3/4". $195-350.

A five tier tree with a rhinestone (43) garland. Each tier uses a light green wash and is slightly raised. There's a cutout area between each tier and a red star at the top. 2-5/8" x 1-3/4". $65-85.

A more recent tree with a green enameled body. A tiny gold rope crisscrosses the tree and red, blue, and amber colored stones (10) sit at the edge. 2-1/2" x 1-3/4". $75-85.

An antique gold, open frame filled with eight rows of red (24) and green (27) stones. This is a tree with real sparkle. 2-5/8" x 2-1/16". $95-150.

Here are five wavy tiers of brushed gold supporting red (4) and green (11) stones in two sizes sprinkled over the tiers. 2-3/16" x 1-7/8". $85-135.

An unusual tree with rope garlands separating the tree into seven tiers. Decorations are red round stones (13) and navettes (4). 2-1/2" x 2-1/8". $65-80.

A brushed gold tree of three tiers with a contemporary look. Stones (7) are vibrant in color and different in shapes and sizes. 2" x 1-5/8". $65-85

A new design using red and green pear-shaped stones in a stacked pattern with aurora borealis rounds between them. 2-15/16" x 2-1/2". $75-85.

Similar to the preceding tree but in four tiers. It is larger with more colored stones (11). 2-5/8" x 2-1/16". $85-125

Gina Wheeler
1994~2002

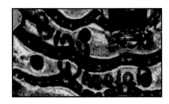

Each of these trees is cast metal and decorated with a theme. They are each hand signed on the back. All of her pins come on a card which reads, "Gems by Gina." They are made in Nashville, Tennessee.

Fisherman's Tree. 2001. $20-35.

English Bulldog Tree. 2001. $20-35.

Christmas Tree. 2001. Approximately 2-7/8" x 1-3/8". $20-35.

Wright Designs
1990 ~ 2002

Wright Designs

In 1970, using wire only, David Wright made his first kinetic sculpture. Twenty years later, after many requests, he crafted his first earrings. Now he designs an eclectic assortment of jewelry colored with special paints and the use of heat. "The ability to accessorize is what separates us from the lower forms of life." —David Wright.

Three Christmas tree designs: The first one 2-1/4" x 2-1/16". $25-35.

2-1/4" x 2-1/8". $25-35.

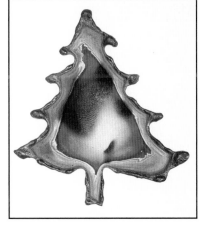

2-1/2" x 2". $25-35.

Zarah Co.
1990 ~ 2002

Gary Schulburg started this company in 1990. Its holiday line was created in 1995. By 1999, Zarah Co. had designed three Christmas tree pins.

Zarah Co. sterling silver enameled Christmas tree signed by artist Linda Bolhuis. 1999. 1-3/4" x 1-1/4" $45-55.

Zarah Co. sterling silver tree signed by artist Judith Geiger. 1999. 2-1/16" x 1-1/4". $45-55.

Zentall
1995 ~ 2002

An old cast tree in a design which looks like "pick-up-sticks" in green wash with two green, two red, and a gold enameled balls. 1-7/8" x 1-1/8". $60-75.

Part 2
Partridge & Pear Tree Pins

"On the first day of Christmas my true love gave to me,
a partridge in a pear tree..."

—Traditional Christmas Carol

The special category of Christmas pins with designs representing the partridge in a pear tree have become highly collectible, too. Examples with the following markings are included here:

Accessocraft
Art
B.J.
Beatrix
Benedikt NY
Cadoro
Catalano
Corel
Gerry
Hagler
Hallmark
Hobé
J.J.
Kirk's Folly
LIA
Mexico
Mylu
Robert
Tancer II
Trifari
Vero
von Walhof
Unmarked

Accessocraft. 2-3/4" x 2-1/4". $60-75.

BJ. 2-1/2" x 2-7/8". $20-35.

Art. 1-3/4" x 1-7/8". $40-50.

Benedikt NY. 2-7/8" x 1-7/8." $75-90.

Beatrix. 1-3/4" x 2-1/16". $45-60.

Cadoro. 2-7/8" x 1-7/8". $90-110.

Cadoro. 2-3/4" x 2-1/8".
$100-150.

Cadoro. 2-7/8" x 1-3/4".
$100-150.

Cadoro. 2-1/2" x 2-1/16". $55-65.

Cadoro. 2-3/4" x 2-1/4".
$150-180.

Cadoro. 1-3/4" x 1-7/8". $40-55.

Corel. 2-1/2"x1-1/2". $45-65.

Cadoro. 2-1/4" x 1-3/4". $40-55.   Cadoro. 1-1/2" x 2". $50-65.

Corel. 1-15/16"x1-5/8". $35-50.

Gerry. 2-3/4" x 1-1/2". $20-35.

Catalano. 2001, 5-1/2" x 4-1/4". $750-1000.

Hallmark. 1-3/8" x 1-1/4". $20-35.

Hagler. 2-1/4" x 2-3/8". $110-125.

JJ. 1-7/8" x 1-7/8". $35-50.

Hobé. 2-3/8" x 1-1/2". $40-65.

Hobé. 2-1/2" x 1-3/4". $60-75.

Kirk's Folly. 3-3/4" x 3-3/4". $225-250.

Kirk's Folly. 3-1/4" x 2-3/8". $50-65.

JJ. 1-7/8" x 1-7/8". $35-50.

LIA. 2-3/8" x 1-3/4".
$25-40.

Mylu. 2-1/2"x2-1/8". $40-65.

LIA. 2-1/4" x 1-3/4".
$45-60.

Mylu. 3-3/8" x 1-7/8".
$65-75.

Mexico Sterling. 2" x 1".
$50-65.

Original by Robert.
2-5/8" x 1-1/2".
$95-125.

Original by Robert.
2-3/4" x 2-1/4".
$135-150.

Original by Robert.
2-3/4" x 1-1/2".
$75-125.

Original by Robert.
2-5/8" x 1-1/2".
$125-150.

Tancer II. 1-7/8" x 1".
$100-150.

Original by Robert.
1-15/16" x 1-5/8".
$135-150.

Trifari. 1-3/4" x 1-3/8".
$70-95.

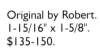

Vero. 1-1/2" x 1-5/8". $25-35.

Unmarked. 1-1/2" x 1-3/8". $40-50.

von Walhof. 4-3/4" x 3-1/8". $165-350.

Unmarked. 1-5/8" x 1-1/4". $35-50.

Unmarked. 2-1/8" x 1-3/8". $35-50.

Unmarked. 1-1/2" x 1-1/16". $10-20.

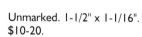

Unmarked. 2-1/8" x 1-7/8". $25-35.

Unmarked. 2-3/8" x 1-7/8". $25-35.

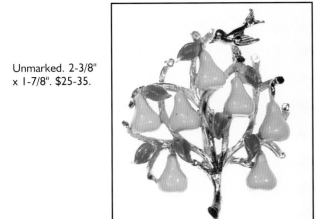

Unmarked. 2-3/8" x 1-7/8". $25-35.

Unmarked. 2-3/8" x 1-5/8". $30-40.

Unmarked. 1-7/8" x 1-7/8". $25-35.

Unmarked. 2-5/8" x 1-3/4". $20-35.

Unmarked. 2-1/2" x 1-3/8". $25-35.

Unmarked. 2-1/4" x 1-3/8". $20-30.

Unmarked. 2-3/8" x 1-7/8". $35-50.

Unmarked. 2-3/8" x 1-7/8". $25-35.

Part 3
Flat Stamp Christmas Tree Pins

The special category of Christmas tree pins made by flat stamped metal and enameled designs are highly collectible because they are fun to find and wear. Examples with the following markings are included here:

All American Pin Co.
Coca Cola
Disney - Michael Co.
Disney - Tokyo
Gift Creations
Hard Rock Cafe
H&H Co.
Jayne Co.
Jonathan-Gray & Assoc.
Olly - Sydney 2000
TEC, Tom & Jerry
The March Co.
United Feature Syn.
USF Inc.
US Secret Service
Warner Bros.
Wincraft, Snoopy

Coca Cola. 1-1/4" x 1-1/4" $7-10.

Disney. 1" x 1-1/4". $7-10.

All American. 1-1/2" x 1". $10-15.

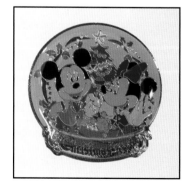

Disney. 1-1/4" x 1-1/4". $5-7.

Gift Creations. 1" x 7/8". $5-10.

Hard Rock Cafe. 1-1/2" x 1-1/4".
$20-25.

Hard Rock Cafe. 1-1/2" x 1-1/2".
$40-50.

H &H Ind. 1-1/4" x 1".
$5-10.

Hard Rock. 2-1/4" x 1".
$20-25.

Jayne Co. 1-1/4" x 1". $5-10.

Jayne Co. 1-1/4" x 1". $5-10.

Jayne Co. 1-1/4" x 1". $5-10.

Jayne Co. 1-1/4" x 1". $5-10.

Jayne Co. 1-1/4" x 1". $5-10.

Jonathan-Gray & Assoc.
1-1/2" x 1". $10-15.

Jayne Co., 1-1/4" x 1". $5-10.

2000 Sydney Olly Olympics.
1-1/4" x 1-1/4". $7-10.

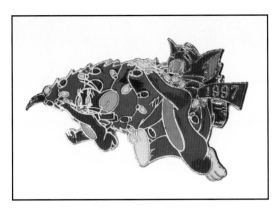

TEC, Tom & Jerry 97. 1" x 1-1/4". $7-10.

98 U S Secret Service. 2-1/4" x 1". $20-25.

The March Co. 1-1/4" x 1-1/8". $40-50.

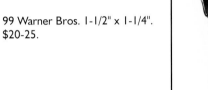

99 Warner Bros. 1-1/2" x 1-1/4". $20-25.

1978 United Features Synd. 1" x 7/8". $5-10.

1958 Starline for USF.Inc. 1-1/2" x 1-1/2". $40-50.

Wincraft Entertainment. 1-1/4" x 1". $5-10.

Bibliography

Books

Baker, Lillian. *Fifty Years of Collectible Fashion Jewelry* 1925-1975. Padducah, Kentucky: Collector Books, 1986/1997.

Ball, Joanne Dubbs. *Costume Jewelers, The Golden Age of Design.* Atglen, Pennsylvania: Schiffer Publishing Ltd, 1990/1997.

Ball, Joanne & Dorothy Torem. *Masterpieces of Costume Jewelry.* Atglen, Pennsylvania: Schiffer Publishing Ltd, 1996.

Becker, Vivienne. *Rough Diamonds* (The Butler & Wilson Collection). New York: Rizzoli International Publications, Inc., 1991.

Dolan, Maryanne. *Collection Rhinestone & Colored Jewelry.* Iola, Wisconsin: Krause Publications, 1998.

Ellis, Kathleen, Ed. *Brand Name Trademark Guide 1994 12th Edition.* Radnor, Pennsylvania: Chilton Co., 1994.

Ettinger, Roseann. *Popular Jewelry of the 60's, 70's & 80's.* Atglen, Pennsylvania: Schiffer Publishing, Ltd, 1997.

Gallina, Jill. *Christmas Pins Past and Present.* Padducah, Kentucky: Collector Books, 1996.

Greindl, Gabriele. *Gems of Costume Jewelry.* New York: Abbeville Press, 1990/1991.

Morrison, Mary. *Christmas Jewelry.* Atglen, Pennsylvania: Schiffer Publishing Ltd, 1998.

Rainwater, Dorothy T. *American Jewelry Manufacturers.* Atglen, Pennsylvania: Schiffer Publishing Ltd, 1998.

Rezazadeh, Fred. *Costume Jewelry, A Practical Handbook.* Padducah, Kentucky: Collector Books, 1998.

Romero, Christie. *Warman's Jewelry 2nd Edition.* Iola, Wisconsin: Kraus Publications, 1998.

Russel, Lynn Ann & Sandy Fichtner. *Rainbow of Rhinestone Jewelry.* Atglen, Pennsylvania: Schiffer Publishing Ltd, 1996.

Schiffer, Nancy N. *Rhinestones! 2nd. Edition.* Atglen, Pennsylvania: Schiffer Publishing Ltd, 1993/1997.

Simonds, Cherri. *Costume Jewelry.* Paducah, Kentucky: Collector Books, 1997.

Articles

Cooney, Joycann. "A Taste of Elegance," *Accessories*, August 1997.

Flood, Kathy. "O Christmas Tree," *Collectibles,* Vol. 8 (4), Winter 2000.

Flood, Kathy. "Pining for Christmas Tree Pins," *Mary Englebreit's Home Companion*, December & January 2000.

'Jewelry designers pick Ulster for work force stability's skills," *Hudson Valley Business Journal*, 9 November, 1998.

Lando, Ruth. "Style Makers 2000: Bettina von Walhof," *Sarasota Style: A Magazine of the Herald Tribune*, November 2000.

Lunch At The Ritz. *Our History:Spring/summer Menu.*1999.

Park Lane. *Realize Your Best With Jewels by Park Lane.*1999.

Pearl International Headquarters. *Erwin Pearl: Timeless Fashion Jewelry.* 2000.

Pitman, Ann. "Christmas Pins are always in season for collectors," *Antique Week*, December 1998.

Pitman, Ann. "Pinning hopes on the goodwill season," *Antique Week*, Vol. 33 (39), December, 2000.

Roman Inc. "Corporate History," (Internet), October 1999.

Stringham, Dottie and Pat Seal. "Illusion Jewels: Costume Jewelry Designers and Companies," (Internet), July 1999.

Tempesta, Lucille. "She has a way with animals," *Vintage Fashion & Costume Jewelry*, Vol. 11 (2), Spring 2001.

Todaro, Sandra. "What's new at a Piece of the Rainbow," *Vintage Fashion & Costume Jewelry*, Vol. 4 (1), Winter 1994.

Index